IMPACT OF DOPPELGÄNGER BRAND IMAGE ON INDIAN PREMIERE LEAGUE (IPL)

About the Book

This is a path breaking book - it takes your understanding of Brands, Brands Maps, and Brand Personality to a new high. The destination however is beyond brands into the realm of Doppelgänger analysis and implications. The author takes you on a journey of laying down the fundamentals of Doppelgänger, leading onto how exactly to quantitatively measure a brand's Doppelgänger. Research Method includes sample, variables, procedure for data collection, various statistical and analytical tools, interview, nature of interview, pre-testing of the tools, primary and secondary data sources, administration of tools, data processing and various precautions undertaken while data collection. The methodology chosen in the research is the Brand Concept Mapping Technique by John, Loken, & Monga, (2006). According to this qualitative technique, respondents were asked to elicit the brand associations linked to Indian Premier League (IPL). The responses by the consumers were to open- ended questions (e.g., What do you think when you think of IPL?). Open-ended question was particularly used to encourage an elaborate and meaningful answer, according to the respondents' own knowledge, experience and/or feelings. Eventually, the book shares the toolkit to apply Doppelgänger methodology to any other brand - and the author aspires this proliferation to be taken to 10,000 more brands. The consequences are materially significant, as the brand custodians would get a powerful perspective on how differently to manage the bands the own, and successfully ward off Doppelgänger .

About the Author

Dr. Gaurav Sood is Professor of Marketing & Strategy, at Faculty of Management Studies (FMS), Manav Rachna International Institute of Research and Studies, India. He is a Brand evangelist, researcher, educator, speaker and columnist with a 2-decade practice creating strong brands. He has been an integral part of developing and Managing Brands for Global Corporate in India, Germany and USA. He has carved out a niche as a brand strategist and pioneer in the domain of brand research. He is an alumnus of Amity University (PhD), India, Emerson College (IMC), Boston, USA, Institute of Management Technology (IMT) (MBA), and of Panjab University (MA), India.

IMPACT OF DOPPELGÄNGER BRAND IMAGE ON INDIAN PREMIERE LEAGUE (IPL)

PROF. (DR.) GAURAV SOOD

AMIGA PRESS INC.

DELHI (INDIA)

AMIGA PRESS INC.
H.O.: 28-A, Indra Park, Chander Nagar
Delhi-110051 (India)
Tel.: 011-22504028, +91-98736-57000
E-mail: amigapress@gmail.com
amigapub@gmail.com
Website : www.amigapress.co.in

This edition is published by Amiga Press Inc.

ISBN: 978-93-84533-50-2

First Published 2019

Printed and bound in India by Replika Press Pvt. Ltd.

ACKNOWLEDGEMENT

Foremost, I would like to express my sincere gratitude to my guide Prof. (Dr.) J K Sharma for the continuous support of my Ph.D study and research, for his patience, motivation, enthusiasm, and immense knowledge. His guidance helped me in all the time of research and writing of this book.

Also, I would like to express my deepest gratitude to Prof. (Dr.) Sanjay Srivastava, who accepted my request to become my Co-Guide and without his guidance and persistent help this Book would not have been possible. Immense gratitude is also due to Prof. Sandeep Mann, who has been my sounding wall in thinking through design and analysis of the research.

Last but not the least, I would like to thank my family: my wife Manpreet Sood and son Rohan Sood, who have been unconditionally supporting me throughout this journey.

FOREWORD

Every instant gives us a new world, a brand-new world. In fact, we all are living in a Brands World – replete with old and new brands. Brands are not only influencing our lives but actually to a large extent controlling them. Everything in today's world can be branded and brands are adding immense value to our lives. To understand customers perceptions of brand(s) is a paramount aspect of brand management and Gaurav Sood has critically examined these perceptions. His prime vehicle has been scrutinizing the imagery of the brand, Indian Premiere League (IPL), in his book. IPL is a significant brand in Indian sub-continent, and amongst all cricket playing nations. The brand custodians strive to build a positive perception in the minds of the consumers – they succeed in some and fail in others. As consumers are the start and end of any brand evolution, they make these brands accountable for their action in the market place. So, where brands develop positive perception, they concurrently give rise to the negative connotations too.

Doppelgänger brand image as captured and analyzed in this book comprises of negative perception about the brand in question and in this case, on IPL. Gaurav has picked up the right brand for his study as IPL is mired in controversies giving rise to creation of its doppelgänger. This book is an in-depth biopsy into IPL's Doppelgänger Brand Image is worth studying. The study would yield deeper insights that can be used for better understanding and management of any brand. He has in fact provided ammunition to the marketer who wants to counter a brand's impending demise by coming up with a disruptive ideology and thus tapping a blue ocean of consumers.

Brands are vulnerable as never before as the customers have taken the control through user generated content which spreads like wild fire when uploaded on social media. Perceptions are fogged by culture jammers posting a real danger for the once loved brands. It is paramount for marketers to take control of this monstrous brand doppelgänger image and develop strategies to stop the creation or slow down the growth of this negative imagery phenomenon. I'm sure that there is great learning for academics and corporate world in managing brands that are attacked by the doppelgänger phenomenon. In hands of Dr. Gaurav Sood, his having been an experienced corporate marketer – the treatment the theme has received is incisive. This would help him establish himself as a thought leader in the brand management space. The book that you are about to read will make you understand the creation and management of the brand doppelgänger image in entirety, and leave you with answers to many questions that would arise over the perusal.

Dr. J K Sharma
Head of the Institution,
Amity School of Business

Dr. Sanjay Srivastava
Vice Chancellor
Manav Rachna University

Book Review

1. "Brand doppelgänger is a challenging, complex and equally relevant phenomenon. Dr. Gaurav Sood has done a significant justice in dealing with the subject by analyzing its intrinsic influence over consumer's mind and their intention to purchase. The book is extremely relevant both for academician, practitioner and students alike. It's a book I strongly recommend." – Padamshri Dr. Pritam Singh, Former DG, IMI, Former Director, MDI and Former Director, IIM, Lucknow.

2. "Managing brand in a highly competitive world is of paramount importance for the organizations. Dr. Gaurav Sood's book is a worthy research work analyzing the brand doppelganger of IPL and its impact on brand imagery. Seeing the limited research done on this phenomenon, it is an important piece of work for the business world." – Dr. Prashant Bhalla, President, Manav Rachna Educational Institutions.

3. "Dr. Gaurav Sood's book takes deeper foray into the phenomenon of Brand Doppelgänger Imagery. His research to test this phenomenon on Indian Premiere League has some surprising outcomes." – Dr. Sanjay Srivastava, Vice Chancellor, Manav Rachna University.

4. "To measure the impact of Brand Doppelgänger Image, Brand Concept Mapping is an appropriate tool. What singled out his research was the potency of its reportage." – Dr. J K Sharma, Director, Amity School of Business.

5. "Dr. Gaurav Sood's research and its application is helpful to all the marketers and future researchers. This book is going to contribute to the theory and practice of brand management and marketers will take inspiration from his ideas to manage their brands. – Dr. N C Wadhwa, Vice Chancellor, MRIIRS.

6. "It's a path breaking research and a revelation in consumer psychology and brand management. Brand imagery is of paramount importance to academicians and industry and this book captures the consumers perceptions regarding the most popular sporting event of India – The IPL. Gaurav has taken the research in the area of brand doppelgänger forward through this book. – Dr. N K Chadha, Chairperson, Doctoral Program, MRIIRS.

7. "Many business books are written with the intention of discrediting conventional business practice and heralding a revolutionary new philosophy…but few succeed. The book "Impact of doppelgänger brand image on Indian premiere league (IPL)" by Dr. Gaurav Sood is an important contribution to the knowledge of branding and a must-read business book". – Anurag Batra, Chairman & Editor in Chief - BW Businessworld.

8. "When you research a brand like IPL and the controversies surrounding it, you need to go deeper into analyzing customer choices. Dr. Sood's book has captured the essence of IPL brand and the impact of its doppelgänger." – Pradeep Magazine, Sports Author.

9. "Prof. Sood's writing on the Brand doppelgänger is insightful. He has researched the concept well and have applied the learning which will benefit both the academicians and practitioners." – Dr. Amit Kapoor, President & CEO of India Council on Competitiveness

10. "Brand IPL is huge. It's power, what it represents and a very public journey of highs lows and controversies, makes it a very interesting subject for investigation. It can teach us something new about brand management. The Brand doppelgänger phenomenon, and the subject of IPL together combine to create an Insightful and interesting must read." – Dev Amritesh, Managing Director India at Compass Group.

11. "Brands have been struggling to the challenge of its own doppelgänger for years. Well measuring the impact and the stage of the brand doppelgänger is a difficult task. In this book, Dr. Gaurav Sood has given a new dimension to the measurement of this monstrous phenomenon. – Manu Nanda, President & Managing Director, Meyer India.

❐

PREFACE

Managing brand image and brand equity has been of paramount importance for marketers and researchers alike. There is a constant face-off between objectives brand custodians pursue and the reactionary customers' perception of a brand. There is a constant hunger for better insights into brand management and corresponding tools and frameworks for reconciliatory platforms. The contrarian strands voiced by Doppelgänger Brand Imagery hold phenomenal potential, so far latent, towards the same. These Doppelgänger Brand Images entail pulling down perceptions that impinge the life cycle and potency of a brand. This Book was set up in the context of empirical evaluation of the Doppelgänger Imagery for a powerful brand, IPL (Indian Premier League), a cricketing extravaganza. Based on robust methodology extending the Advanced Brand Concept Maps, the research explores and assesses the dynamics of a brand at all levels: listing of impacting constituents, their relative importance, and the drift of their positive or negative influence, et al. Very interesting outcomes have arisen, which shall enable analytic measurement of a brand's potency, factoring all of its key influencers, inclusive of the Doppelgänger ones, as emanating from various communities or segments of customers. This research thus paves way for threadbare mapping of every brand so that it can contest the negative imagery and emerge strengthened.

Chapter I underline the concept of Brand Doppelgänger Imagery and its impact on overall brand performance. The strong underlining idea in this case is the importance of brand and its relationship with its consumers where people buy brands and not products and brands connect with consumers on a psychological level. Further there is a gap between how marketers communicate the brands and how consumers finally consume. This gap creates confusion and leads to positive as well as negative associations in the minds of the consumers. The negative associations are than circulated by the consumers on the popular culture and takes the form a monstrous doppelgängerbrand imagery. This doppelgänger imagery is the double of the existing brand but behaves in a negative way. Since the case in point in our research is Indian Premier League (IPL), therefore it was essential to identify the negative associations linked to this international sporting extravaganza. The positive and negative associations are than plotted on a brand concept map and the strength and uniqueness of these associations are than analysed on an individual and at an overall network level. The chapter gives a theoretical knowledge about the concept of brand doppelgänger along with the way it can be measured.

Chapter two is devoted to the review of the literature summarises brand as a concept, brand imagery, anti-branding, culture jamming doppelgänger, brand image, Indian Premier League (the case in point) etc.. It is based on scholarly articles, books etc written by experts in the field of brand; the idea is to find the current researches on the topic and finding gaps if any. As such, it is a prelude to further research, a digest of scholarly opinion. This chapter emphasizes on the secondary data and literature review. The experts' view on the creation of Brand Doppelgänger and tools and techniques of measurement is shared. The literature was searched through various Indian and International journals and books written by eminent subject specialists. The literature review takes a deep dive into the genesis and creation of the doppelgänger image and its impact on the performance of the brands. It also looks into the various dimensions of brand image with respect to the IPL tournament.

Chapter three is devoted to the research methodology used to carry out the research work As defined by business dictionary, Research Methodology is, "The process used to collect information and data for the purpose of making business decisions. The methodology may include publication research, interviews, surveys and other research techniques, and could include both present and historical information."

Research Method includes sample, variables, procedure for data collection, various statistical and analytical tools, interview, nature of interview, pre testing of the tools, primary and secondary data sources, administration of tools, data processing and various precautions undertaken while data collection. The methodology chosen in the research is the Brand concept Mapping Technique by John, Loken, & Monga, (2006). According to this qualitative technique respondents were asked to elicitate the brand associations linked to Indian Premier League (IPL) based on the responses by the consumers to the open-ended questions (e.g., What do you think when you think of IPL?). Open-ended question was used to encourage an elaborate and meaningful answer according to the respondents' own knowledge, experience and/or feelings.

Further, the consumers plot the brand associated network map and then the brand concept maps are created by aggregating the individual maps. The network of brand associations shows how strongly and uniquely the brand associations are connected to each other and with the core brand. Further the research analyze the value of the brand association network (BANV) – a quantitative techniques to gauge the favourability or purchase intent of a particular brand association individually and the favourability of the overall network of associations.

Chapter four discusses the findings, results and analysis including both qualitative & quantitative measures to analyse the data used in the study. It focuses on having an open view about the knowledge and implementation of Brand Doppelgänger Imagery. The research analyzes the frequency of mention of each association, number of interconnection each association has, the first-order association frequency of occurrence, Ration of first-order association and brand associations subordinate and superordinate associations connections. We followed a 5 step process to aggregate the individual maps and develop a consensus map. Frequency and number of interconnections were the measures used after identifying the core association of IPL. The core associations were identified from the individual maps where the associations with more than 50% of mention was chosen as core associations. The second step was to build the consensus map by linking the core associations with IPL on the basis of their frequency of mention and the association links frequency in the individual map. The 3rd step involved plotting the association remainder on the map and their links with the core brand associations were positioned on the map. The 4th step involved the addition of important linkages between core and non-core associations. Though the focus generally is on the core brand associations but it is critical to understand the consumer perception that drives the core associations through the non-core associations. The 5th step was to identify the strength of the core and non-core association and the intensity of their linkages through weak (single line), moderate (double lines) and strong (triple lines). The intensity of linkages was decided after calculating the mean value of the no. of lines which are drawn to connect the two associations. After capturing the consensus map we need to satisfy the standard measurement criteria like reliability and validity. We did split-half validity measurement by dividing the consensus map into two halves. This was followed up by the known group approach to conduct the nomological validity. Further we calculated the brand association network value (BANV) in order to quantify the overall favourability The chapter have given a directional framework for the interpretation and conclusion to the conducted research.

Chapter five discusses the drawn results and associates them to the designed objectives of the research. Various tools such as Brand Concept Maps etc have been used in the chapter to draw the conclusions with highest possible validity & reliability. All the 25 brand associations have been critically examined to draw directional results.

Chapter six represents the conclusion, recommendations, limitations and other related aspects of the research. The implications of the study have been mentioned in detail and remedial measures to cater the various aspects of the brand Doppelgänger have also been discussed.

Dr. Gaurav Sood

TABLE OF CONTENTS

CHAPTER - ONE

AN OVERVIEW OF THE DOPPELGÄNGER BRAND IMAGE

INTRODUCTION

The history of branding goes back to the early nineteenth century. During those times, all we could understand was that advertising and branding were same, were tantamount or overlapping. But gradually dawned the realization that actually they are completely different facets and processes of business and economic life. Advertising is merely a subset of branding – branding is the supra-umbrella. Mid of the nineteenth century saw the first of the mass marketing campaigns - the objective was to inform the consumers about the attributes of the product. Gradually the advertisers realized that the advertising does not only inform, but more importantly also generate feelings. Therefore the marketers shifted their focus from the physical aspects of the product to a mapping of the psychological impact of a brand image in consumers' lives along with its anthropological.

Understanding customers' interpretation of brand image is of paramount concern for both researchers and practitioners of management, business and advertising. As firms strive to boost brand equity and gain/ maintain competitive advantages, the aforementioned become paramount. Brand equity and brand value are widely discussed in extant studies (for example, Aaker, 1996; Keller, 2003; Lassaret et. al., 1995). Professor Jean-Noël Kapferer in 1986 was the first person to come out with the concept of "Brand Identity". He developed a brand identity six-sided prism model, which explained the six aspects of brand identity into two dimensions.

The first dimension talked about brand as a person and can be explained as brand physique and brand personality and also depicts user reflection conjoined with and self-image. Second dimension explained a brand's social aspects; its physique, relationship and reflection integrated into the brand personality. According to Kapferer, "Strong brands are capable of weaving all aspects into an effective whole in order to create a concise, clear and appealing brand identity" (Kapferer, 2012). Brand has been the cynosure of most academicians and marketing professionals – a concept revered and even defined multifariously. Nevertheless, its centrality cannot be overemphasized if one has to conceive or initiate marketing initiatives. Brand is by definition associations, which form a network in the mind of its consumers (Keller, 2003). Higher the brand equity, higher are the consumer preferences and intentions to buy (Cobb-Walgren, Ruble & Donthu, 1995). Also, brand equity when high leads to higher stock returns (Aaker and Jacobson, 1994). While Keller (2003) gave the pathway to build brand equity; a conceptual framework to map customer based brand equity was given by Fayrene and Lee (2011). Kuhn (2008) attempted to apply Keller's (2003) B2B branding for commercial and industrial contexts.

Further, imagery based on anthropomorphisation (perceiving the human in forms and events which are not humanlike, suffuses human appraisals (Guthrie 1995)) of products has been a powerful concept; Aggarwal and McGill (2007) have offered a framework to understand the phenomenon of anthropomorphisation of products. They concluded that the consumers positively evaluate products that are presented as humans and have physical characteristics like human beings. Anthropomorphisation portrays a brand as an analogue of man, having a structure or morphology akin to a human being. Brown's (2010) pitch for anthropomorphisation seems very convincing as the best recourse to a larger market share. This is due to a more likely adoption of the brand by marketers and advertisers when the image chosen is an animal, which is "closer" to humanity. However, Holt (2010) has shown how anthropomorphism makes the branding indefensible and even irrelevant for the consumers. He has pioneered the Cultural Strategy Book, while diagnosing failure of brands. He has in fact provided ammunition to the marketer who wants to counter a brand's impending demise by coming up with a disruptive ideology and thus tapping a blue ocean of consumers.

Despite efforts by marketers to promote their brands and influence consumers' consumption pattern, there has always been a conflict between how companies market their brands and how consumers at large consume/ perceive the brand. Consumers in most of the cases tend to resist the marketers influence over consumers' consumption pattern change. Because of this resistance to change, brands try to target their messages again and again and at every touch point of consumer engagement. They believe in both percussion/ frequent hammering, as also varying point of attack. Thereby, there is always consumer tendency to increase their buying power and erode marketers control over their consumption habits or life. According to Claudy, Garcia, & O'Driscoll, (2015), "Consumer behavior frameworks in diffusion of innovation (DOI) studies have largely failed to distinctly account for reasons against adoption. Indeed, no study to date has tested the relative influence of adoption and resistance factors in a single framework."

Also since most of the brands are selling online and their marketing budgets are increasing in the digital marketing space; thus it is easy for consumers to create content and culturally jam the brand messages. According to Fournier, S., & Avery, J. (2011); "These strategies present a paradox, for to gain coveted resonance, the brand must relinquish control. We discuss how Web-based power struggles between marketers and consumer brand authors challenge accepted branding truths and paradigms: where short-term brands can trump long-term icons; where marketing looks more like public relations; where brand building gives way to brand protection; and brand value is driven by risk, not returns."

Brand image constitutes the most vital element of brand meaning creation in the minds of the customer (Keller, 2003). Grasping totality of brand image is few strong, unique, and favorable associations of the brand in consumer's mind in the form of network of associations (John, Keller, 1993, Kim, & Monga, Loken, 2006;). The brands associations' networks indicate towards the direct linked associations (core associations) or indirect linked associations to the brand and also indicate mutual connect between these brand associations. Naturally, network of associations are a good correlate of a brand's value to consumers (Aaker, 2010; John et al., 2006).

As the literature and advertising thought dipped into generic and universality of brand and brand image, alongside arose concepts of negative brand Imagery, esp. as a Doppelgänger brand image. The Doppelgänger as a concept originated from the German Romantic literature and became a widely accepted subject matter in the "Gothic" literature. The Doppelgänger terminology first was cited in the novel Siebenkiis by Jean Paul, published in the year 1796 (cited in: Vardoulaki 2006). According Thompson, Rindfleisch & Arsel, (2006), "Doppelgänger Brand Image is a family of disparaging images and stories about a brand that are circulated in popular culture by a loosely organized network of consumers, anti-brand activists, bloggers, and opinion leaders in the news and entertainment media."

Though negativity around brand has not been studied much; many online spaces encouraging anti-consumption and anti-branding have been mapped (Krishnamurthy 2009). There is a study that sheds some fundamental light on why people avoid a particular brand (Lee 2009). Harold (2004) has talked of pranksters using media activism to provoke brand custodians. Giesler (2012) tried to get insights in Doppelgänger Brand Image via Botox market analysis over an eight-year period. Creation of Doppelgänger Brand Image for strong brands merits worthy fathoming, since the leader brands are likely to be more vulnerable to lose the equity of the brand. The Doppelgänger Brand Image might confuse customers and motivate them to avoid the brand, this is known as "brand avoidance" effects (i.e., consumers intentionally avoid a brand in question) as described by Thompson, Rindfleisch & Arsel, (2006). Therefore, this creation of Doppelgänger Brand Image might lead to negative brand imagery, consumer judgment and consequently impact consumer brand's cultural resonance. According to Freund and Jacobi (2013): "The emergence of a powerful, popular Doppelgänger **may signal that a brand has peaked and must either evolve or decline**." Using Goldman Sachs as a case study, Freund and Jacobi (2013) explored that the generation and circulation of the ugly Doppelgänger brand imagery influence the stakeholder perception of a company brand by anti-brand activists. This lineage of how organizational personae are created is very insightful.

Thompson, Rindfleisch & Arsel, (2006) integrated Holt's (2010) prime concepts with Doppelgänger Brand Image, showing how the traditionally adopted Emotional Banding lay defunct in face of Doppelgänger Brand Image. As a maverick, Vardoulakis (2006) has given a brave contra-rendition, in delinking Doppelgänger with demonic, in fact showing it as having a potential of positivity. **This positivity facet is intriguing and requires further study.**

Studies on brand image are based on consumer perceptions rather than on any rigorously tested measures (Lassar, W., Mittal, B., & Sharma, A.,1995). Aaker (1996) has delineated ways to measure brand, indicating how such a complex construct like brand can be practically measured. Ways to measure Doppelgänger Brand Image have been discussed by Brandt, Pahud de Mortanges, Bluemelhuber & Van Riel, (2010) by studying negative user-generated content. Schnittka, Sattler & Zenker, (2012) have validated Brand Concept Maps, John, Loken, Kim & Monga, (2006) as most appropriate measuring mechanisms.

Doppelgänger Brand Image, an emerging concept in this body of literature, holds tremendous potential for deeper forays. Doppelgänger Brand Image is a set of negative perceptions that influence the effect of a brand in consumer's perception (Giesler 2012). The proposed research aims **to study the impact of creation of Doppelgänger Brand Image on brand imagery**; this is well nigh a less explored space. This impact would be measured by systematic and diligent application of rigorous Advanced Brand Concept Mapping network associations (Schnittka, Sattler & Zenker, 2012). The research not only attempts to identify varied sources of creating a Doppelgänger Brand Image, but also identifies **empirically deciphered potency** of these influencers in creating the same.

The specific brand chosen for this study is Indian Premier League (IPL), an international cricketing event hosted by India. Studies have explored IPL as a global brand (Sapna Singh 2012). Singh mapped various beliefs/approaches of branding the IPL teams. According to Sapna, Indian Premiere League (IPL) is a composite of cricket packaged in entertainment. Gupta (2011) has brought in a chronological build-up of brand IPL, showing how the IPL model has controlled the world cricket. Further, he cautioned about problems associated with the game (financial scams, match fixing scandals, favoritism, players off-field involvements etc.). Edelman, D. C. (2010) concludes "the IPL is a 'disruptive' development for world cricket and has changed the nature of the sport in significant ways."

Over past, cricket has traditionally been a game played by gentlemen; but IPL is involved in dirty spats of fixing the matches and bad governance, exposing the dark side of the game. These have given rise to IPL's Doppelgänger Brand Image. Hence, a deeper diagnosis into IPL's Doppelgänger Brand Image is worth researching. The research will bring out some deeper insights that can be that can be applied to various other brands. Thus this brand, which has a big stature and brand robustness, because of its materiality and institutionalization, makes a worthwhile center of the proposed research study.

CONCEPTUAL FRAMEWORK

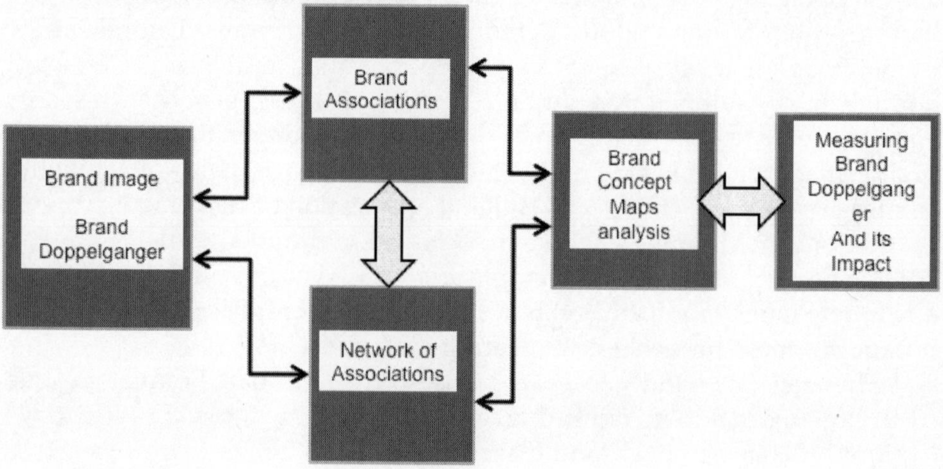

Figure 1

The conceptual framework was developed keeping into consideration the genesis of the Doppelgänger image phenomenon and how it takes a monstrous position and damages the imagery of a particular brand. Further this historical evolution of the Doppelgänger brand imagery has emerged from the very existence of the positioning of the brand and can be rooted in the very communication, messaging and mental mapping of the brand. A brand is multidimensional and its linkages and dimensions are worth a study to understand this negative imagery phenomenon called brand Doppelgänger leading to the destruction of a brand. Therefore, to gain better understanding of the imagery of a brand, brand equity, anti-brand activities and cultural jamming concepts became the creator of the brand Doppelgänger phenomenon. The research took a deep foray into these concepts and their impact on the brand with a special emphasis on the rise of the anti-brand activities through stakeholder generated content and activism through offline and digital media particularly the likes of facebook, twitter etc. We also researched the risk associated with the mindshare, emotional and cultural strategies and how through cultural jamming consumers/competition can pull down a brand from a higher ground position. We took a deep dive into lots of brand case studies, books, research papers etc. to understand the approach of the marketers in creating a mouse-trap for consumer buying. One of these concepts was "Mind-share strategy" to develop a consumer mouse-trap. Therefore when brands adopt a mind-share strategy their brand communication is targeted to gain the maximum share of consumers mind space with abstract concepts like "Khushion ki home delivery", "Fanta is FUN", "Youngistaan" etc. The mind-share (a bridge between the functional and emotional benefits) approach implies that consumers value these abstracts and hence are more loyal to brands. Brands rely on these abstract positioning as it is easy to develop, understood and measurable but they are also vulnerable to backlash by consumers for creation of Doppelgänger imagery.

While mind-share and mousetrap strategies have been replaced by emotional and cultural brand strategies but still are vulnerable to consumer backlash resulting in brand Doppelgänger. Where emotional brand strategy is more consumer oriented and relates to consumers inspirations, aspirations and delivers the message in the form of story telling picking up cues from consumers situations and life circumstances. Thompson, Rindfleisch, & Arsel, (2006) argues that; "emotional-branding strategies are conducive to the emergence of a doppelgänger brand image, which is defined as a family of disparaging images and meanings about a brand that circulate throughout popular culture." They further go on establishing the proposition that brand doppelgänger could help the brand warning it in advance and a corrective brand strategy can be used for brand's advantage. Referring to Starbucks, they were able to justify the need of understanding and analyzing brand doppelgänger image and how proactively it can be used for a brand's advantage.

On the other hand the cultural branding strategies propagate leaving the red ocean of intense competition and finding a blue ocean through cultural expression. Holt (2010) argues "The engine of cultural innovation is historical change in society that is significant enough to destabilize the category's cultural orthodoxy, creating latent demand for new cultural expressions." Therefore a social disruption can make a brand leader loose and other takes off because of understanding this social change and capitalizing with the right cultural expression. There are many examples like PayTM, Maggie, PVR, IPL etc.

Since brand image is the network of associations, therefore our research focusing on understanding the brand image components through a network of brand associations. Brand associations are the associations deep rooted in the minds of the consumer and therefore needs to be surfaced through the elicitation technique, which is the foundation of developing the brand concept maps. Brand Concept Maps are further used to plot these associations in a network map and the strength; uniqueness of these associations needs to be analyzed. Further we measured the impact of the negative doppelgänger associations and how they influence the favorability of the purchase intent. Though the BCM approach limits itself to analyzing the favorability and strength of the brand associations, therefore it was essential to analytically quantify the direction or the favorability of the network of associations towards consumers purchase intent.

The conceptual framework was developed after rigorous research to understand the genesis of the doppelgänger brand image and identification of the methodology to capture the negative imagery and to analyze the negative associations behavior in the overall network of associations. Therefore while researching the negative associations of IPL, we researched the overall growth in brand value of IPL and the impact of its' doppelgänger imagery on the brand IPL. Over the years IPL has evolved as a international cricketing tournament and has received a celebrity tournament space like Wimbledon etc. Lots have been written and spoken about the game and due to IPL's emotional connect to the tune of fanaticism, it has drawn lots of negative publicity due to controversial events revolving around the game. Since IPL's brand value and fan following is cutting across all demographics particularly the youth and is rising year on year (YOY), therefore it was essential to develop a research framework which could capture the brand associations linked to IPL and analyze the impact of the positive as well as negative association in the overall context of the IPL brand imagery.

ORGANIZATION OF Book

The Book focuses upon an empirical research on the Impact of Brand Doppelgänger Imagery. The main components associated with the research covers different IPL brand associations and their impact on the overall brand performance.

The introduction of the Book underline the concept of Brand Doppelgänger Imagery and its impact on overall brand performance. The strong underlining idea in this case is the importance of brand and its relationship with its consumers where people buy brands and not products and brands connect with consumers on a psychological level. Further there is a gap between how marketers communicate the brands and how consumers finally consume. This gap creates confusion and leads to positive as well as negative associations in the minds of the consumers. The negative associations are than circulated by the consumers on the popular culture and takes the form a monstrous doppelgänger brand imagery. This doppelgänger imagery is the double of the existing brand but behaves in a negative way. Since the case in point in our research is Indian Premier League (IPL), therefore it was essential to identify the negative associations linked to this international sporting extravaganza. The positive and negative associations are than plotted on a brand concept map and the strength and uniqueness of these associations are than analysed on an individual and at an overall network level. The chapter gives a theoretical knowledge about the concept of brand Doppelgänger along with the way it can be measured.

The entire research study has been categorized into seven important chapters, the brief of which has been presented as follows:

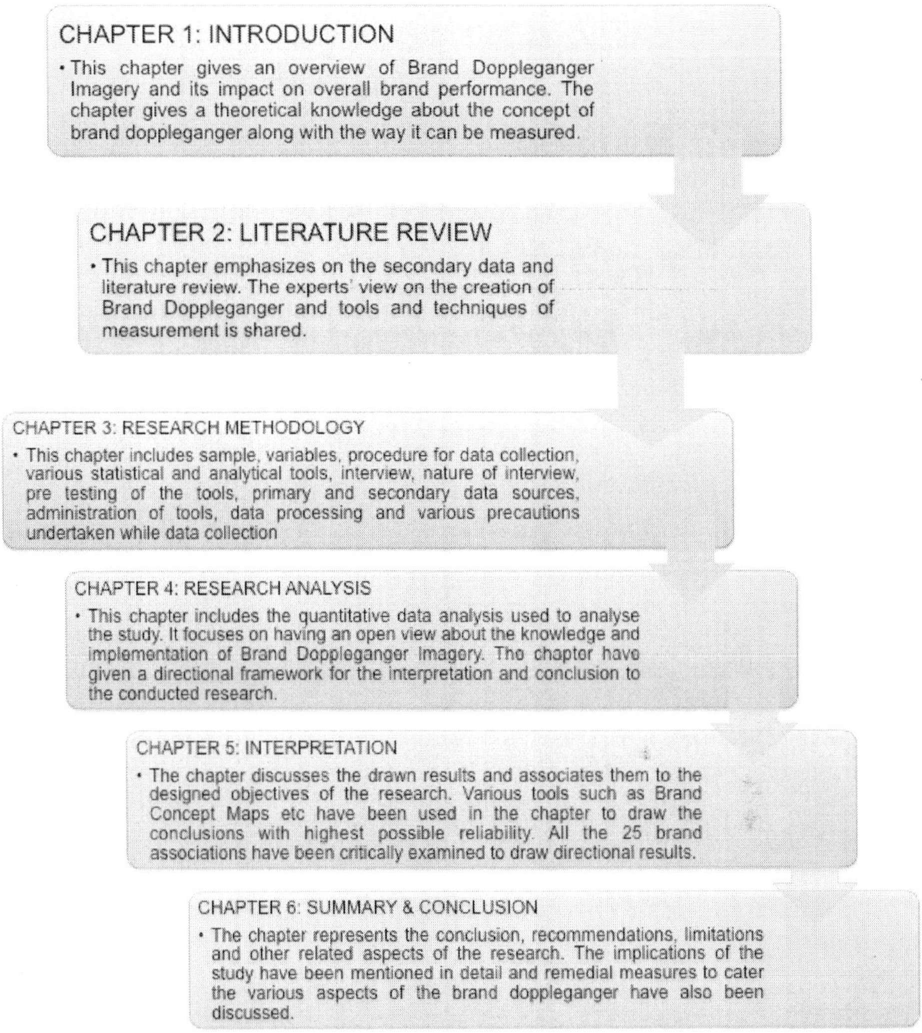

Figure 2

The review of the literature summarises brand as a concept, brand imagery, anti-branding, culture jamming, doppelgänger brand image, Indian Premier League (the case in point) etc.. It is based on scholarly articles, books etc written by experts in the field of brand; the idea is to find the current researches on the topic and finding gaps if any. As such, it is a prelude to further research, a digest of scholarly opinion. This chapter emphasizes on the secondary data and literature review. The experts' view on the creation of Brand Doppelgänger and tools and techniques of measurement is shared. The literature was searched through various Indian and International journals and books written by eminent subject specialists. The literature review takes a deep dive into the genesis and creation of the doppelgänger image and its impact on the performance of the brands. It also looks into the various dimensions of brand image with respect to the IPL tournament.

As defined by business dictionary, Research Methodology is, "The process used to collect information and data for the purpose of making business decisions. The methodology may include publication research, interviews, surveys and other research techniques, and could include both present and historical information."

Research Method includes sample, variables, procedure for data collection, various statistical and analytical tools, interview, nature of interview, pre testing of the tools, primary and secondary data sources, administration of tools, data processing and various precautions undertaken while data collection. The methodology chosen in the research is the Brand concept Mapping Technique by John, Loken, & Monga, (2006). According to this qualitative technique respondents were asked to elicitate the brand associations linked to Indian Premier League (IPL) based on the responses by the consumers to the open-ended questions (e.g., What do you think when you think of IPL?). Open-ended question was used to encourage an elaborate and meaningful answer according to the respondents' own knowledge, experience and/or feelings.

Further, the consumers plot the brand associated network map and then the brand concept maps are created by aggregating the individual maps. The network of brand associations shows how strongly and uniquely the brand associations are connected to each other and with the core brand. Further the research analyze the value of the brand association network (BANV) – a quantitative techniques to gauge the favourability or purchase intent of a particular brand association individually and the favourability of the overall network of associations.

Research analysis includes both qualitative & quantitative measures to analyse the data used in the study. It focuses on having an open view about the knowledge and implementation of Brand doppelgänger Imagery. The research analyzes the frequency of mention of each association, number of interconnection each association has, the first-order association frequency of occurrence, Ration of first-order association and brand associations subordinate and superordinate associations connections. We followed a 5 step process to aggregate the individual maps and develop a consensus map. Frequency and number of interconnections were the measures used after identifying the core association of IPL. The core associations were identified from the individual maps where the associations with more than 50% of mention was chosen as core associations. The second step was to build the consensus map by linking the core associations with IPL on the basis of their frequency of mention and the association links frequency in the individual map. The 3rd step involved plotting the association remainder on the map and their links with the core brand associations were positioned on the map. The 4th step involved the addition of important linkages between core and non-core associations. Though the focus generally is on the core brand associations but it is critical to understand the consumer perception that drives the core associations through the non-core associations. The 5th step was to identify the strength of the core and non-core association and the intensity of their linkages through weak (single line), moderate (double lines) and strong (triple lines). The intensity of linkages was decided after calculating the mean value of the no. of lines which are drawn to connect the two associations. After capturing the consensus map we need to satisfy the standard measurement criteria like reliability and validity. We did split-half validity measurement by dividing the consensus map into two halves. This was followed up by the known group approach to conduct the nomological validity. Further we calculated the brand association network value (BANV) in order to quantify the overall favourability The chapter have given a directional framework for the interpretation and conclusion to the conducted research.

Chapter five discusses the drawn results and associates them to the designed objectives of the research. Various tools such as Brand Concept Maps etc have been used in the chapter to draw the conclusions with highest possible validity & reliability. All the 25 brand associations have been critically examined to draw directional results.

Chapter six represents the conclusion, recommendations, limitations and other related aspects of the research. The implications of the study have been mentioned in detail and remedial measures to cater the various aspects of the brand Doppelgänger have also been discussed.

❐

CHAPTER - TWO

LITERATURE REVIEW

Philip Kotler defined brands as helping people to make decisions. In a world of fierce competition and consumer empowerment, brands can influence consumers' perception and help make them a choice. Brands are what people buy to make a difference in their lives. Brands affect the individual or group of individual's decision-making process and create a positive impact on the consumers' intention to buy. Brands define consumer's personality, culture and beliefs.

Brands are intangible and are embedded in the minds of the consumers. They add value in consumer's life and create a strong resonance leading to strong customer-based brand equity.

BRAND AND BRANDING

Brand is a complex phenomenon. Though brands have been of interest to both marketers and academicians alike, but brand experts are the ones with set philosophy circulating the brand. "Each expert comes up with his or her own definition of brand or nuances of definition" (Kapferer, 2012), which compounds the complexity in alternate interpretations of brand and also its management. (Kapferer, 2012), Brand Prism is a useful tool for marketers to develop the brand identity through different stages of execution (offline & online).

David Aaker too pronounces, "...there are two ways to compete. The first, to win the brand preference competition by making a brand preferred over other brands in an established category or subcategory, is tough and expensive. The second, to win the brand relevance competition by creating new categories or subcategories for which competitors are irrelevant, is a route to growth and profitability."

Furthermore, a brand's positioning is being continually assailed; sustaining relevance necessitates customer engagement in methods, which are perfectly authentic. This is the most complex aspect of brand management these days. Big brands have to face this challenge perennially.

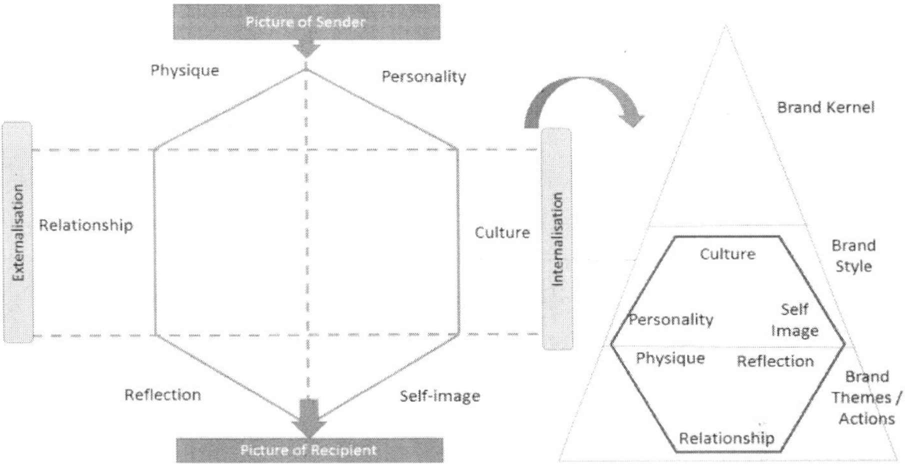

Fig. 3. Brand Prism, from "Strategic Brand Management", by J. N. Kapferer (2002).

The brand prism concept has been developed for the success of any brand in order to establish a unified image in the minds of the consumers. Brand prism has six facets, which represents the brand identity.

- **Physique** – The physical or tangible aspect of a brand defines the personality of a brand. The logo, colour, packaging etc. are the tangible aspects of a brand and they help in establishing brand's personality and identity in the consumers' mind.
- **Personality** – Brand communication sets the tone for any brand, this tone of voice defines the brand personality, e.g. Confidence tone of voice, advisory tone of voice etc.
- **Culture** – The values that define the culture of the brand like the reference culture for the origination of a brand (country of origin).
- **Relationship** – Brand has to establish a relationship with the consumer and give a reason for purchase.
- **Reflection** – The target audience who could be the possible consumer/user of the brand and the situations/circumstances they might choose to consume the brand.
- **Self Image** – Every brand needs to fulfill an aspirational need of the consumer.

Though the marketers create the identity of a brand, meaning to a brand is created by the consumers, Batey, M. (2015). To understand brand meaning it is essential to understand consumer behavior and their motivation that drives them towards a particular brand. Now, understanding consumer motivation requires a need to understand their motivation to buy and their motivation to consume separately. The lacuna in understanding consumer motivation to buy is to emphasize on rational choices which consumer makes. Though brands address the rational part of the consumer behavior but it is more targeted towards the irrational semiconscious emotional needs and unconscious physiological requirements of the consumers. The American Marketing Association defines Brand and Branding as "A brand is a customer experience represented by a collection of images and ideas; often, it refers to a symbol such as a name, logo, slogan, and design scheme. Brand recognition and other reactions are created by the accumulation of experiences with the specific product or service, both directly relating to its use, and through the influence of advertising, design, and media commentary." "A brand often includes an explicit logo, fonts, color schemes, symbols, sound which may be developed to represent implicit values, ideas, and even personality." Brands are valuable to corporates and stay as long-term assets with the company. Therefore it is important that corporates need to define the relationship between brand loyalty and brand value as part of the management accounting system, Wood, L. (2000). Also brand equity is an asset because it defines the trust, which consumers bestow in the brand (Delgado-Ballester, & Luis Munuera-Alemán, 2005). Therefore higher the trust, higher is the equity of the brand.

Branding is not a key component for the tangible product but also a key element of the service marketing too, Berry, L. L. (2000). On the pivotal issue of how the brand strategies can be developed, Chernatony and Williams, (1989) talk of two key components characterizing brands and through the use of a two dimensional matrix, thus identifying the type of brand. Now brands need to be strong, for that is where business has competitive advantage. Hoeffler and Keller (2003) show how strength of brand, can lead to different set of responses towards different marketing initiatives by consumers.

Though there are many definitions of the brand but most of them fail to define the theory of a brand and its dimensions, De Chernatony & Dall'Olmo Riley, (1998) tried to define a brand. They identified categorizes brand construct into 12 main themes, from a broad range of brand definitions, i.e. as:

(i) Brand as a Legal entity;
(ii) Brand is as good as it's logo;
(iii) The company is the brand;

(iv) Brand is a shortcut to functional & emotional response;
(v) Brand reduces risk;
(vi) Brand adds identity to a product;
(vii) Brand = Brand Image;
(viii) Brand has defined values;
(ix) Brand has a Personality too;
(x) Brand builds relationship;
(xi) Brand adds value to the top & bottom line; and
(xii) Brand is an evolving entity.

The categorization into the 12 themes captured the essence and meaning of the brand from various sources that defined the concept.

A brand is a perceptual quintessence that is deep down establishes deeply and firmly subjective perceptions and further the odd behavioral components of consumers. Finally a brand is perception or network of associations that stays in the mind of consumers. Trout, J., (1969), coined the term Positioning - as perception in consumer mind. Ries, A. and Trout,J. (1981), in their book "Positioning: The Battle for Your Mind", elaborates on the concept positioning as creating a position in the minds of the customer. The positioning reflects a brand's SWOT – Strength, Weaknesses, Threat & Opportunities vis-à-vis competition. There are many techniques to capture the consumers' brand perception like Spidergram, Intuitive Maps, perception maps etc. The most common used technique is the perceptual map, which diagrammatically displays the perception of the consumers relative to the competitive brands in the industry. Perceptual maps reflect the brand position in the mind of the consumer in a form of a graph with X & Y axis formed by product attributes (Kardes, F. R., Cronley, M. L., & Cline, T. W., 2011).

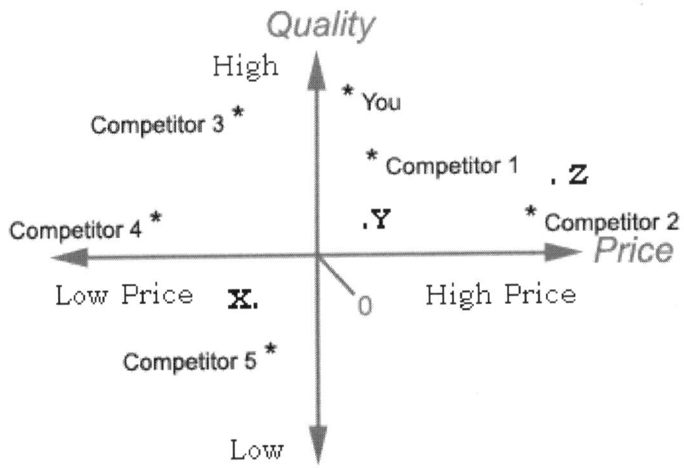

Fig. 4 From "Brand Positioning", by Subroto Sengupta (1990).

Traditionally a brand is generally referred to product & services has and branding is the process which has been associated with attaching intangible meaning to the products and services, but branding has now been associated with entities such as people, places, things, ideas too. Off lately branding has been used to market social causes and has faced with lots of challenges. Social marketing is a process to change perception and behavior of consumers at large to benefit the society or nation. Though in branding of products the return on investment is tangible, whereas in social branding the return on investment in exchange of the response of the consumer is intangible and long-term, Keller, K. L. (1998). Branding of sporting event involves building relationships with consumers through strategic engagement at each consumer touch points. Sports events are using social media more effectively than ever to engage their target audience and build strong brand equity in the digital space. Brands which have high visibility on the social media channels are more likely to be preferred by the consumers. Watkins, B. (2014), studied the influence of social media on brands and how consumers' identify and build relationships with the brands on social media leading to a strong brand equity. Taking NBA as a case study the research concluded that the brands which have a strong social media presence particularly facebook & twitter have better consumer engagement.

According to Aaker (2012), "A key to building strong brand is to develop and implement a brand identity." He further goes on differentiating brand image with brand identity, according to him brand image is about how consumers' perceive a brand and brand identity is how the company wants the consumers to perceive the brand. So, companies are always working towards bridging the gap between brand image and identity as they strive to match the two.

An interesting study of Good Brands Doing Bad has been there by Aaker, Fournier & Brasel (2004). They studied the relationship between the consumers' and the brand and how it evolves into a great relationship. The relationship with the sincere brands or serious brand personality post purchase goes wrong whereas in the case of exciting brand personality it's the other way round..

Traditionally brands were communicating their messages through offline media and with the revolution of the digital media brands are capitalizing on the social media to reach out to their target audience. According to Barreda, Bilgihan, Nusair & Okumus (2015), "With their exceptional interactive and communicative capabilities, Online Social Networks (OSNs) allow destinations and companies to heighten their brand awareness". Social media has redefine how brands have to be marketed and how consumers will consume. According to Van den Bergh, J., & Behrer, M. (2016), "In today's world of social media, with an explosion of touch points, an overload of choice on product and service offerings, and with purposeful Millennial, people don't buy brands – they buy into brands". Therefore it is essential for marketers to include digital media in their marketing mix and engage consumers on social media platforms. "The Internet is changing all the rules of branding, except one—creating an emotional bond with buyers is still essential." - Travis, D. (2001).

Branding in a digital age is a challenge for today's marketers, the traditional branding paradigm focused on profits by way of heavily investing in media buying with controlled communication. But in today's digital age according to "However, social media can drastically alter consumers' behavior and their brand preferences. This rapidly evolving landscape has left managers at a loss, and what they are experiencing is likely the beginning of a tectonic shift in the way brands are managed". No marketers can think of marketing their brand without brand's digital presence as the digitally empowered customer, is a key role player in brand building, (Rowley, J., & Edmundson-Bird, D., 2013). The way consumers connect and engage with brands digitally is often not in the control of the companies. Therefore the classical models of marketing and branding need to be redefined to adapt to the new age brands.

A digitally empowered buyer systematically make his digital journey to select the brand of his choice and completes his decision making journey with a purchase according to his own choice. Further a consumer not only finishes his engagement with the brand or company of choice but continues to remain engaged with the brand on social media after the purchase too.

Therefore marketers need to study this new branding paradigm of "consumer decision journey" for their brands and tailor made their brand-consumer engagement strategies to win the customer. Edelman (2010), published a paper in Harvard Business Review and has thrown some spotlight on the "Consumer Decision Journey" in the age of digital branding.

Fig. 5. Consumer Decision Journey - From "Branding in the Digital Age", by David C. Edelman (2010).

In the offline or traditional consumer-buying journey, consumer use to narrow down their brand alternatives after careful research and than use to buy it. The relationship with the brand was strong before or at the time of purchase and than would have been limited to the use and service of the product in order to reduce their cognitive dissonance.

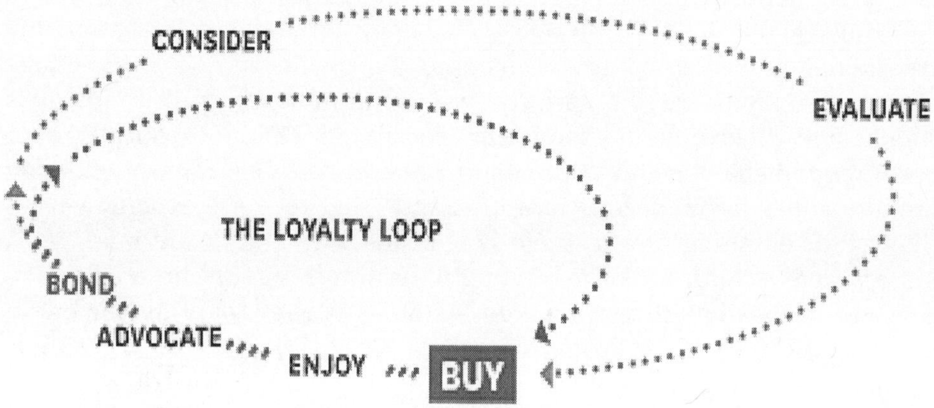

Fig. 6 "Loyality Loop"-From "Branding in the Digital Age", by David C. Edelman (2010).

But in the digital age the consumer enters into a dialogue with the brand in an open-ended relationship platform and voices their opinion and experiences on social media. A good brand review can enhance the image of the brand and a bad one can spell disaster due to consumer backlash on the social media.

BRAND IMAGE AND BRAND EQUITY

Brand image is the consumers' assessments and imagery in mind of a user/ buyer. Brand Image is a set of brand associations, anchored firmly in the minds of the consumers. It defines the beliefs and existence of the brand. Marketers use this imagery to position their brands in consumers' mind.

Brand image is the set of brand associations gathered by consumers from various sources.

Brand image strongly influences the consumer purchase decision as it represents the emotional aspect of a brand (Arora & Stoner, 2009). Consumers not only buy a product for a logical reason but also for the brand imagery associated deep down in his/her mind. Different authors have interpreted brand imagery differently. According to the American Marketing Association (AMA) definition brand signifies "name, term, design, symbol, or any other feature that identifies one seller's good or service as distinct from those of other sellers," whereas brand image by definition is a "perception of a brand in the minds of consumers. It is what people believe about a brand – their thoughts, feelings, expectations" (AMA). Aaker (1992) defines brand image as a "set of associations, usually organized in some meaningful way" whereas Keller (1993) defined it as a "perceptions about a brand as reflected by the brand associations held in consumer memory".

Brand image is a key component of brand equity as it represents consumers' beliefs, ideas and impression about a particular brand. Brands continuously try to influence the consumers' perception about their brand and therefore establishing a strong brand imagery. While Dobni and Zinkhan (1990) take on brand image is as follows:

- "Brand image is the concept of a brand that is held by the consumer.
- Brand image is largely a subjective and perceptual phenomenon that is formed through consumer interpretation, whether reasoned or emotional.
- Brand image is not inherent in the technical, functional or physical concerns of the product. Rather, it is affected and molded by marketing activities, by context variables, and by the characteristics of the perceiver.
- Where brand image is concerned, the perception of reality is more important than the reality itself."

Brand image is all about the perception of the customer. Further, Associative network theory is identified as the basis for researching brand image. Researchers like (Aaker, 1991; Biel, 1993; Keller, 1993; Roth, 1995; Hsieh, 2002) have developed the brand association constructs based on associative network model. It is a well-established fact that the consumers' brand knowledge affects their purchase decision. Therefore it is required to measure the brand knowledge of consumers.

Brand associations as looked through the eye of the beholder were reported by Grace, D., & O'Cass, A. (2002). The absence of empirical testing was challenged; from viewpoint of brand practitioners. The researcher used qualitative methods to look up the main dimensions of a brand such as core product/service, experience with brand, image of user, which are significant/ critical to consumers. Facets like feelings, and self-image were important for branded products, while word-of-mouth, employees referrals, were vital for service brands.

On the other side, Brand equity is a vital facet of brand, and it originated in 1980s. Brand equity has a deep relation with brand loyalty and brand extensions. Therein arises the challenge of determining content and measurement of brand equity - whether financial or customer-based. The customer-based brand equity was studied by Chieng and Goi (2011). Faced with absence of business-to-business (B2B) branding framework, Keller's model of customer-based equity' was applied in a B2B context

Kuhn, Alpert & Pope (2008) - indicating higher emphasis for selling organization's corporate brand and its staff curability. Keller (2003) enabled insights into various relationships that accrue, due to brand linkages to people, places, things, or other brands, in order to influence their brand equity. Drawing a relationship between the marketing elements (product, price, place & promotion) and brand equity Yoo, B., Donthu, N., & Lee, S. (2000), suggested that more the advertising, better the product benefits, premium pricing and extensive distribution leads to higher brand equity.

Keller, K. L. (2001) in his working paper introduced the Customer Based Brand Equity (CBBE) model and how it is a blue print for creating strong brands. Kellers' CBBE pyramid model is about four fundamental questions the consumers of a particular brand will invariably ask. The first question represents the first stage at the bottom of the pyramid of the CBBE model about the brand identity and awareness to the consumer at large. The customers should be in a position to identify various elements of a brand, which are uniquely different from other brands. The second stage comprises of the performance and imagery of the brand. The third stage is about the judgment and feelings about your brand i.e. what does the customer think or feel about your brand? Customers generally give emotional response to a brand and are constantly judgmental about how a brand makes them feel about themselves. Keller (2003) has identified 6 brand feelings (fun, excitement, warmth, security, social approval, and self-respect).

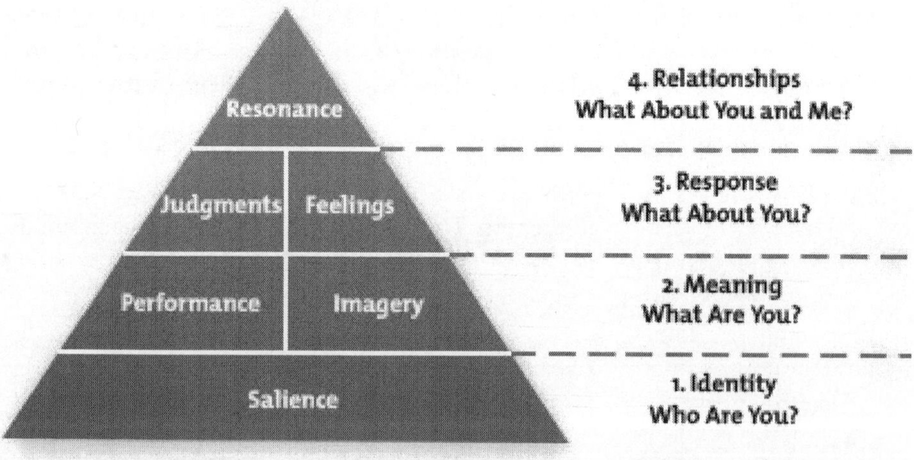

Fig. 7 CBBE Pyramid - From "Strategic Brand Management: Building, Measuring, and Managing Brand Equity" by Kevin Lane Keller.

The fourth and most important stage is Brand "resonance" at the apex of the CBBE pyramid 'cause every brand wants loyal customers. Brand resonance/loyalty is when customers develop a deep psychological bond with the brand and repeatedly buy the product.

The importance on branding in the overall marketing strategies by the marketers in particular, in red ocean – fiercely competitive market, marketers leverage secondary brand associations to other entities, like, people, places, things, or piggy back on leader brands, in an effort to improve their brand equity. In order to understand this leveraging of the secondary associations process by the marketers it is critical to understand the influence & impact of secondary brand association on consumer brand knowledge and how it can be changed. According to Keller, K. L. (2003), "adopting broader, more holistic perspectives that synthesize the multidimensionality of brand knowledge is critical to advance branding theory and practice, both in general and with brand leveraging in particular." Further stating on the importance of brand equity Menon, V. P., & Barani, G. (2016) stated "brand managers should consider the relative importance of brand equity in their overall brand equity evaluation and should concentrate their efforts primarily on perceived quality and brand loyalty."

Brand image on digital media is trickier to analyze as the electronic word of mouth relevance and involvement with the issue is the key motivator for someone to re-tweet a positive or a negative content, B Barhorst, J., & Wilson, A. (2017). Brand associations and brand loyalty are the key components of brand equity and they have a strong influence on the purchase intention. (Jalilvand, M. R., Samiei, N., & Mahdavinia, S. H., 2011). Though individually brand X may have a strong brand associations than brand Y but the brand loyalty of brand Y may be higher than brand X in the same case.

ANTI BRANDING

Brand is no doubt a dynamic asset and it simply can't stay static. Thereby, its negative dimensions may flare up. In this linkage delving into theories of consumer resistance, and so coming forth with an alternative model, it has been shown that brands are authentic cultural resources (Holt, 2002). Anti-brand behaviors have been observed to be diverse: from customers' complaints, to negatively talking about the brand, to adopt illegal means to register their protests. Mapping was done as to understand the conditions, which lead to such relationships that may harm the very existence of the brand. (John, Loken, Kim & Monga, 2006). Consumer may develop a negative disposition towards a brand but that is more likely to happen after the relationship has ended. At this stage the consumer might get engaged in anti-brand activities especially when the relationship is low on self-relevance. (John, Loken, Kim & Monga, 2006). The anti-brand activism at times originates from the moral corruption of the brand or the company and it is stronger in the case of low consumer empathy towards the brand. (Romani, Grappi, Zarantonello & Bagozzi, 2015).

Hogg (1998) explored the phenomenon of avoiding a brand (brand avoidance), and its determinants. So as to keep brand flexible enough to remain workable. Further, Light was shed on the process of learning in negotiating brand meaning within the community of anti-brand consumers (Hollenbeck & Zinkhan, 2010). It was revealed that brand meaning is a process of engagement of a community in brand discussions, message interpretations, making sense of brand meaning.

Media and communication environment has under gone a transformation. Transformation creates change through collective efforts of the individuals. Thus, in digital space, where individuals are more empowered and are in a advantageous position to learn, communicate, and collaborate more than ever, and are far better capable of bringing in impactful change. (Sivitanides, M., & Shah, V., 2011). In recent times, there has been a paradoxical situation between anti-brand and brand structures. (Østergaard, P., Hermansen, J., & Fitchett, J., 2015). This paradox leaves the consumer confused as to which direction to go and whom to trust.

Anti-brand can't be completely said to have been studied, unless the Internet dimension has been covered. Brand activists target web sites. Digital media has witnessed growth of the anti-consumption activism but its impact on the brand has not been measured till now. (Krishnamurthy, S., & Kucuk, S. U., 2009). The marketing's anthropomorphic propensity, via brand animals, mascots and icons is an interesting study, which develops brand strategies based on the brand icons life cycle (Brown, S. 2010). Emotional branding is hugely in currency, even though this strategy is beset with many risks. Rindfleisch, A., & Arsel (2006) reasoned that emotional-branding strategies are vulnerable of a doppelgänger brand image, which is defined, "as a family of disparaging images and meanings about a brand that circulate throughout popular culture". The primal Book they proposed was that a doppelgänger brand image can dilute the intensity of an emotional-branding story.

Negative Double Jeopardy (NDJ) was researched by Kucuk (2008): that the most valuable brands are attacked more through the anti-brand sites than the less popular ones. The NDJ phenomenon and the NDJ components [' Brand Rank ' and ' Brand Consistency '] were thus introduced. Negative PR can lower consumer perceptions of a brand. Analytic thinkers most probably are less and less dependent on transferring negative information to the parent brand. This is through accordingly (Monga and John, 2008). Berger, J., & Milkman, K. L. (2013) studied the positive effects of Negative

PR, where such negative publicity actually increased the sales. Common sense indicates all publicity is good publicity. However, prior research had revealed only negative press demerits. Employing econometric analyses and experimental methodologies, these viewpoints were to outline contexts under which negative PR can have positive as well as negative effect. Therefore, negative PR should have different effects on known and unknown brands.

Kucuk, S. U. (2016), tries to develop a relationship between the brand hate and anti-branding through various general psychology and behavior literature. He tries to define the concept of brand hate and degree of its components. According to him there are two components of hate as per the literature of psychology – "threatened egotism" and "perceived injustice" and the intensity of hate depends on how low or high these components behave, (Kucuk, S. U., 2016). Further he proposes that marketers should listen to and engages with the anti-brand activists or so called brand haters to negotiate with them in order to have a peaceful solution for a healthy brand-consumer relationship. Since brands are going social, therefore for our understanding we should treat social media as a telephone and not as a megaphone. Which means that there is a two-way communication and not a monologue on social media between brand and its consumers. Brands need to listen to their consumers through various social media listening tools like Hootsuite, tweetreach, Klout etc. The success on social media depends on how effectively you make the most of the social media by listening to your customer, competitors and consumer at large. You should know what the audience has to say about you on the social media platform and how they are engaging with you and your competition. Once you know what the brand haters are saying about you by sabotaging your messaging, it will be easy to develop a strategy to gain competitive advantage through strong social business intelligence. Managers need to cope up and strategies for the risks created by the anti-brand attacks and how they can weave it in with their CSR initiatives. (Kay, M. J., 2006). Further the consumption choices, buying behaviour of consumers are under constant contest creating cultural tensions. (Luedicke, M. K., & Giesler, M., 2008). The negative consumer reactions, which leads to moral brand conflict is framed by the myths created by the moral protagonist and consumers use these myths to develop a Doppelgänger identity of the brand. (Luedicke, M. K., Thompson, C. J., & Giesler, M., 2009).

CULTURE JAMMING

One of the stratagem in negative attack is parody. Jean (2011) studied the measurement of the implication of parody on brand attitudes, which are victim of brand parody. This study demonstrated that the fun-twist of a brand by anti-commercial style of negative humor is dangerous for a brand. Going deeper in this arena, studies have mapped popular culture and modem communications media. It goes beyond mass media (Guillory, 2010). An across the spectrum exploration of cultural jamming was done from a point of view of developing a theoretical approach to explaining behavioral change and tactical choice (Iles, 2013). What came up was a rigorous conceptualization of culture jamming as an oppositional tactic.

Cultural jamming, a key part of negative branding, was linked to prankster (Harold, 2004). It was indicated the pranksters aren't revenge prone, instead they are on a provocative mode. "Culture jamming' is defined as 'an organized, social activist effort that aims to counter the bombardment of consumption-oriented messages in the mass media" (Handelman and Kozinets, 2004: n.p.). Carducci (2006) took this further to fathom sociological perspective on culture jamming. Cammaerts (2007) extended the cultural jamming techniques' appropriation by political actors in their political communication practices. These 'political' jams are very different from the culture jams and are not targeted towards the corporates. They are up in arms with the establishment and the society at large.

Naomi Klein (2000) takes an aim at the brand bullies in her best seller "No Logo". Referring to big brands like; Microsoft, Nike, Wal-Mart, Starbucks etc., she discusses the backlash these super brands have faced owning to culture jamming. Naomi Klein (2000), defined culture jamming as follows: "culture jamming is the practice of parodying ads and hijacking billboards to drastically alter their messages." "Something not far from the surface of the public psyche is delighted to see the icons of corporate power subverted and mocked," Though from culture jamming impact on the social and political set up, it has significant economic effect also. According to Carducci, V. (2006), "An analysis of culture jamming needs to supplement sociological examination with a consideration of its political and economic effects. To be truly effective as a cultural, media, and social practice, it appears that culture jamming must be tied to a larger purpose and not be taken as an end in itself."

Technology advancement has empowered customers and has exposed brands to extreme nature of culture jamming through social network. According to Naomi Klein (2000), "Culture jamming is enjoying a resurgence, in part because of technological advancements, but also more pertinently, because of the good old rules of supply and demand. Something not far from the surface of the public psyche is delighted to see the icons of corporate power subverted and mocked."

While online, some people can afford to live dual life like Dr. Jekyll and

Mr. Hyde. In his book Stevenson, R. L. (1927), scripts the dual personality, which is morally different from each other. Our Internet gives this freedom to the trolls to express their Mr. Hyde syndrome when online. People behavior changes while being online, they will act in a different way online than they would do in a real life situation. Suler, J. (2004), introduced concept called "The Online Disinhibition Effect" and identified six factors that lead to change of people's behavior when online. These factors, which are responsible for a person's new emotional and experimental dimensions while online, are as follows:

1. Internet gives you anonymity
2. Internet makes you invisible
3. Internet not a real-time interaction
4. It's all in the users head
5. Internet as a dream virtual reality
6. Minimization of authority

The status of anonymity and invisibility a person enjoys online makes him say things, which he will not say otherwise and also gets away with it.

These troll not only culture jam the communication but also can create a Doppelgänger brand imagery.

According to Dery, M. (1993), culture jamming has many forms:

1. Sniping and Subvertising
2. Adbusters
3. Media Fake News
4. Audio Propaganda
5. Billboard Banditry
6. Guerrilla Semiotics
7. Postscript from the edge

Marketers have considered consumers as the King but when consumers wear the citizen glasses than the consumption becomes political. In the case of Nike Sweat-shops, Peretti, J., & Micheletti, M. (2011), the political consumers challenged the corporate policy of using child labor to produce Nike shoes. Well, the problem Internet faces is the communicative nature of the digital medium, McCaughey, M., & Ayers, M. D. (Eds.). (2013). Internet not only becomes a two way medium but also gives freedom to consumers to express their opinion or pass judgments on the brands or the company and culture jam their messages through cyberactivism.

Sandlin, J.A. (2007), referred culture jamming as a critical public pedagogy, which engages learners, is poetic in nature and creates community politic by connecting individuals to the society at large. Culture jamming is a form of pedagogy, which incorporates participative communication strategies to jam the culture, Milstein, T., & Pulos, A. (2015).

There is a shift from consumer activism to consumer hacktivism (Hearn, Mahncke & Williams, 2009). People use Internet to promote their political ideologies in order to disrupt the communication. The issue of hacking, a new kind of Internet threat, was studied to show how disrupting communications using Internet enabled networks and organizations was done. (Mahncke & Williams, 2009). The hackers are technically hacking to shield the dominance practices of their respective countries. This is akin to civic engagement in international relations (Jordan & Taylor, 2004). The complete spectrum historical context of hacktivism is laid out in terms of new social movements. This shows the direct action and its contribution to the globalization dialogue.

Foundation of semiotic theory primarily by Ferdinand de Saussure and Roland Barthes, conducted on the related issues of Culture Jamming as a social phenomenon was done by (**Önal**, 2005). Rumbo (2002) was the brains in showing inversion of resistance into an advantage - the barricades in launching challenges to consumerism over cultural spaces were studied. It was demonstrated how marketers have steered resistance efforts from some of consumption's most bitter critics into useful market segments by targeting specific goods and services toward them.

Shimp T. (2013) gave a revolutionary Book on pranking, illustrating how the yes man culture instilled culture jamming and carried tones of a disruptive rhetoric. Specifically, this Book poses many research questions, key ones being: What rhetorical strategies do the Yes Men use to critique dominant corporate discourse and expose counter discourses? A Foucauldian rhetorical analysis reveals that the Yes Men rely on pranks that employ satire and sincerity to disrupt dominant corporate discourses, open spaces of freedom, and encourage critical self-reflection. The strategies of the Yes Men offer no doubt important insight into the relationship between rhetoric, discourse, and activism.

Darts, D. (2004) in his paper, Visual Culture Jam: Art, Pedagogy, and Creative Resistance, contends that that visual culture is prime component for art educators who study social justice issues and promote democratic principles through their teaching. The study analyses how visual culture education can empower students to see and meaningfully engage in the ideological struggles fixated in the daily visual experience.

DeLaure, M., Fink, M., & Dery, M. (Eds.). (2017), examines the phenomenon of culture jamming by modern day activists in order to bring social change by challenging the status quo. Culture jams do not work in isolation and are not one time stand-alone piece of user generated content but it tears its way into the ongoing brand campaigns and disrupt the brand communication, Klein, N. (2000). Beside the consumer activism to culture jam the brand messages; the competitors are also very active to sabotage the rival brands through brand parody. Jean, S. (2011) tried to analyze the impact of brand parody by competitors on the consumers' attitude towards the brand.

With the rise of social media the word of mouth (WOM) propagation about a brand, issue etc has been faster than never before. The word of mouth publicity of new ideas and products has become a critical component of marketing communication. Any thing in public domain brand, people etc. are facing a continuous WOM through customers' complaints and dissatisfactory tweets or posts. These negative WOMs are the online firestorms, Pfeffer, J., Zorbach, T., & Carley, K. M. (2014) and is a big challenge for the marketing communication department. Further the online firestorms are created through consumer's existing social network.

Gladwell, M. (2006) argues that ideas, behavior, messages and products spread like epidemic and when they reach a critical mass, they become the tipping point. According to him the tipping point is contagious and has dramatically big impact.

Mapping the evolution of the Doppelgänger imagery, Sood, G & Sharma, J K (2016) laid emphasis on the critical dimensions of the Doppelgänger imagery including brand image, brand equity, anti-branding and culture jamming. These dimensions either influence or get influenced by strong Doppelgänger imagery.

Tweets, re-tweets, share etc. are few ways consumers make some campaign go viral. According to Berger, J., & Milkman, K. L. (2013), "Content that evokes either high-arousal positive emotions (awe) or negative emotions (anger or anxiety) tends to be more viral." Berger, J. (2016) further goes on defining the principles for particular things to go viral. Social currency, triggers, emotional resonance, useful information and storytelling are the main principles that drive brands to become contagious. The heroes of culture jamming are the trolls and the bad clowns who threaten the Internet domain by jamming the culture. Bad Clowns, according to Radford, B. (2016) is the ones who spread terror, spread hate and are evil in nature. They mysteriously show their hidden side and troll people, corporates and brands and spread fear all around. These troll according to Shin, J. (2008), are unaware of the behavior morality on the online space as it is devoid of the moral code of conduct as in an offline environment.

DOPPELGÄNGER BRAND IMAGERY

Abi-Ezzi, N. (2000) pores over the representation of the Double in the Book of R. L. Stevenson, Wilkie Collins and Daphne du Maurier. This is with particular reference to The Strange Case of Dr. Jekyll and Mr Hyde', *The Woman in White,* and *Rebecca.* A rejection of the prevailing social order is the basis of this rejection; different in each case that determines the context in which each treats the double. This psychological symbolism manifests itself in several themes - namely the representation of landscape, animals, masquerade and writing - central to the main texts, and relating them clearly to one another. This study, then, while contributing on one level to the comparatively sparse literature on Collins and du Maurier, expands an understanding of the motif of the double by filling a gap in existing criticism, demonstrating that it is to no small degree through the relationship of the double to a given set of themes, defined through psychological symbolism, that the course and fulfillment of its function are explained.

Webber, A.J. (1996), gave the working definition of the term Doppelgänger. According to him Doppelgänger is:

(a) "Double Vision" because it is above all figure of visual compulsion
(b) "Double Talk" because it causes disagreement and creates hostility on language.
(c) A performer of identity representing the other self
(d) A tussle between the ego and the alter-ego
(e) Takes a position opposite to the host
(f) Repeats itself and returns as a uncanny according to Freud
(g) A male
(h) Originate from a dysfunctional family

The word 'Uncanny' is the opposite of the German word 'Heimlich' meaning the 'familiar' or 'known'. Therefore 'uncanny' is the unknown or unfamiliar and that is why it is freighting. (Freud, S., 2004). Conceptual metaphors like Doppelgänger or uncanny can become real and that is the most horrifying thought (Schneider, S., 1999). If we go through the earlier literature on Doppelgänger from the texts from the 1927 book by Stevenson's "The Strange Case of Dr. Jekyll and Mr. Hyde" and the Dostoevsky's "The Double" in 1846, the alter-ego or the evil twin is considered to be the subset of the Doppelgänger. Doppelgänger according to them is a outcome of the ego and alter-ego split. Some definitions point out hat Doppelgänger is different from the alter ego as it may represent doom or death but is not the exact opposite of the self (Fonseca, T., 2006).

The re-emergence of the Doppelgänger phenomenon in the German literature by authors from various generation and origin is symbolic of the social crises before the reunification of the German borders. It also discusses the 'uncanny' as a figure of Doppelgänger (Gilson E., 2013). The Doppelgänger can also be themed as 'disobedient shadow' of the hero, which has an identity of its own and becomes the ghostly double of the hero his master. (Micali, S., 2010). Alfred Hitchcock has used the doppelgänger as a psychoanalytical perspective of the 'other' in his movies. The 'other' represented the 'self' who has been 'doubled' in his many films (de Sousa, R. L., 2012).

Aggarwal, P., & McGill, A. L. (2007) rub it in a satirical way when they query, "Is That Car Smiling at Me?" Their research examines how effective is product anthropomorphism and what is its' consequences. The findings suggested that the consumers capability to anthropomorphize a product depends on the congruence of product characteristics with the human schema.

Sood & Sharma (2016) mapped the evolution of the doppelgänger brand image, according to them "better understanding of the brand and its imagery, equity of a brand, anti-branding and cultural jamming are necessary dimensions to understand the background to genesis of the doppelgänger brand." Giesler, M. (2012)'s paper: "How Doppelgänger Brand Images Influence the Market Creation Process: Longitudinal Insights from the Rise of Botox Cosmetic", uses the theory of sociology – the actor-network theory; exploring the process of creation of new markets as a branding process.

According to Thompson, C. J., Rindfleisch, A., & Arsel, Z. (2006), emotional branding is a successful branding strategy for competitive advantage. They argue that the brands which ride on an emotional-branding strategy are more prone to the creation of their doppelgänger, which is defined as "a family of disparaging images and meanings about a brand that circulate throughout popular culture". According to the authors the doctrine of strategy riding on getting consumers' emotional response through emotional branding leads to creation and propagation of doppelgänger brand imagery. They concluded that a doppelgänger brand image can be positive for a brand and not merely is a threat by giving warning signals that an emotional-branding story is losing its relevance. The emotions, which will determine the future of a brand, are fear and hope (Gobe, M., 2001). Where fear creates panic and hope drives innovation, these emotions decide whether the consumers are going to stay or leave the brand.

Freund, J., & Jacobi, E. S. (2013) analyzed the cultural branding theory through brand psychoanalysis, and literature review and explores the monstrous Doppelgänger brand imagery of Goldman Sachs. They further concluded that the creation of Doppelgänger brand imagery could be due to lack of application of a brand's emotional or cultural branding strategies. In the case of Goldman Sachs evaluated the role of critics in transmuting the brand imagery of an otherwise healthy and successful global bank into monstrous entity. It is evident that brand doppelgänger focus on the negative side of the emotions and pitch against organizations by exposing, anthropomorphizing, and dramatizing their insinuated, monstrous, ulterior ponsee, and effects. This study had a tremendous contribution to the literary concept on brand doppelgänger by underlining the significance of anthropomorphism when the strong brand is attacked, which do not employ traditional (emotional) or new age (cultural) brand strategies.

Zivkovic, M. (2000) assumed Doppelgänger has not originated from the literature but is has emerged from the traditional culture. It is a subversive function appeared from the psychoanalytical theories.

Vardoulakis, D. (2006) elaborates Negation, going onto the Doppelgänger in Freud's "The 'Uncanny'". The Doppelgänger figure is a negative character, which has a split personality syndrome and is devilish and evil in nature. The psychoanalytical tools are able to indicate that a doppelgänger is a sense loosing oneself. The one thing about the Doppelgänger is that it is as a departure from true self. Now, psychological symptoms can be in the literature of the Doppelgänger. The Doppelgänger has an intrinsic property of being expressed as a positive character.

According to Füller, J., Lüdicke, M. K., & Jawecki, G. (2008), developed the concept of "community brands", which are created and driven by the online consumers. The community brands inspire creativity with a freedom of expression in the digital space. Brands generally have fan following and it is these fans who also are responsible if dissatisfied in the creation of the Doppelgänger brand images and are responsible for the destruction of the once followed brand, Parmentier, M. A., & Fischer, E. (2014). With the free access to the Internet and empowered online users, brands are always under the public scrutiny, Gabl, S., Wieser, V. E., & Hemetsberger, A. (2016).

Lee, Z., McCloskey, J., & Beverland, M. (2015), have identified the process of consumers judgment on Doppelgänger brand images. According to them, the consumer journey experiences a four-stage process of judging brand Doppelgänger.

These are:

1. Criteria selected for judgment
2. Search for information
3. Cognitive processing of the Doppelgänger imagery
4. Final judgment through outcomes

DOPPELGÄNGER BRAND IMAGE MEASUREMENT

Keller (2001) stated that brand image is a network of brand associations in the minds of the customers; therefore, it is critical to measure these associations both positive and negative. Low & Lamb (2000) outline the dimensionality and the way brand associations can be measured. The findings of the research explained the relationship between brand association dimensionality and brand familiarity and concluded that the dimensionality of brand associations has a positive correlation to brand familiarity. The purpose of the research is to test empirically the three dimensions: brand image, brand attitude and perceived quality of the brand associations. The study concluded that the brand associations' dimensions are influenced by brand familiarity.

According to Brandt, C., Pahud de Mortanges, C., Bluemelhuber, C., & Van Riel, A. (2010), Brand Image talks of associative networks, which can be a method of capturing Doppelgänger Brand Image. Though the negative user-generated content (UGC) on the Internet can be damaging and easy to viral but less is known on the impact of the destruction caused by the doppelgänger brand image (DBI). The authors define DBI as reinforcement of brand's negative associations by circulating it in the popular culture by its stakeholders.

John, D. R., Loken, B., Kim, K., & Monga, A. B. (2006) explain Brand Concept Mapping techniques, thus yielding a methodology for Identifying According to this methodology the brand associations are identified through elicitation and then a consensus brand map is arrived at through individual brand concept maps of consumers.

Taking the brand concept mapping methodology forward, Schnittka, O., Sattler, H., & Zenker, S. (2012) developed advanced brand concept maps (ABCM). According to John, D. R., Loken, B., Kim, K., & Monga, A. B. (2006) brand concept maps (BCM) methodology is a powerful technique to identify the brand association's strength and uniqueness through the network of brand association technique. Though, BCM, as well as other consumer mapping techniques, fail to identify the favorability of brand associations and its' impact on purchase intensions. The ABCM though has given a Brand Association Network Value (BANV) metric to measure the favorability of the individual and network of brand associations and its effect on the purchase intention.

Thompson, Pollio & Locander, (1994) suggests that brand avoidance by consumers happens when there is gap between the emotional brand promise and the brand performance. Well self-conception plays an important part when brand symbolizes an important meaning in the life of the consumer. Consumers do not forget and forgive when their most trusted brand defaults on its promise. Brands who do not employ emotional branding strategies not necessary loose out to their competitive strategies but brands who are not gained an iconic stature may not be attacked and may escape the anti-brand brigade onslaught.

Christensen, G. L., & Olson, J. C. (2002) maps consumers' mental maps with ZMET. Zaltman metaphor-elicitation technique (ZMET), Zaltman (1997) captures the top of mind brand associations and than develop a mental map based on the consumers' knowledge network about the brand. This helps in capturing the consumers' insights through their knowledge structures by developing the mental models made up of both cognitive (beliefs) and emotional (feelings) components. The consumers' knowledge structure is affected and can be positive or negative based on consumers' current consumption.

Dwelling on the advantages of the ZMET technique, John, D. R., Loken, B., Kim, K., & Monga, A. B. (2006) developed Brand Concept Maps, thus developing the brand association network. They introduced the associative network technique, Brand Concept Maps, and created individual consumer maps of brand associations and derived the consensus brand maps. The BCM is a network of core and other brand associations, which depicts the brand's image and display direct and indirect links between the core and the other brand associations.

Schnittka, O., Sattler, H., & Zenker, S. (2012) went a step ahead and developed and advance BCM approach to measure the brand image. John and others (2006) brand concept maps (BCM) is a powerful technique that capture the strength and uniqueness of brand associations. Where as, the ABCM also captured the favorability of the network of brand associations and hence could define the purchase intent of the consumers. They also were able to quantify the overall favorability of the brand association network by developing Brand Association Network Value.

INDIAN PREMIERE LEAGUE (IPL)

Cricket is the king of all the sports in India, cricket carries millions of fan following, viewership and tremendous loyalty. Cricket is popular across masses of all age group and countries. Cricket in India attracts lots of money in the form of sponsorships, ads etc., it is the most richest game in the country. The most famous cricketing event in the world is no doubt the Indian Premier League (IPL), a shorter format 20-20 overs game.

Sood & Sharma (2015) have captured the essence of IPL and its' Doppelgänger image, according to them, "Doppelgänger Brand Image is a nouveau construct in the studies of brands and brand values. It maps negative perceptions, which impact a brand, as retaliation to its positive persona. This case study traces origination of Indian Premier League (IPL), a powerful sports domain brand in India, and how it has been buffeted by its doppelgänger. The problems within (financial irregularities, match fixing scandals, nepotism, off-the-field conduct of players etc.) have been laid bare. The reader develops a good understanding of the drivers behind the formation of this brand's doppelgänger. The unmanageability of such a fearsome development has been treated akin to birth of a Frankenstein for the brand (Brandenstein)."

Sporting events like IPL and the noise they make can be analyzed through user data on social media. Till now the popularity of a sporting event on social media can be quantified and computed a number of tweets or retweets on Twitter or through calculating facebook likes and shares or pictures posted on instagram but now days the analysis is done by calculating number of tweets normalized by population.

Lakshman, C., & Akhter, M. (2013) investigated the corporate governance issue in the Indian Premiere League (IPL). They argued that the IPL corporate governance model breaded greed and corruption and tarnished the image and the morality of the gentlemen sport. Too much power and no accountability led the break down and mis-management of the overall corporate governance structure of the IPL. This brought bad name to the governing body, players, franchise and sponsors alike. Pepsi even backed out from the main sponsor category. Though Pepsi was the main sponsor and the IPL event sponsorship had a very strategic role in Pepsi's overall marketing communication strategy. People were emotionally connected with the IPL and with the sponsors. Grime, I., Diamantopoulos, A., & Smith, G. (2002) mapped the role of emotions as foundation to events and sponsoring brands. Event sponsorship are leveraged by brands to develop a strong positioning strategy and gain mindshare. The companies sponsor events to gain competitive advantage, they try to piggyback on the sporting property and connect with consumers emotionally. But if the sporting event defaults on ethical values the sponsoring brand also gets a bad name, hence it is a two edged sword for sponsors.

Naik, A. Y., & Gupta, A. (2013) studied the Branding of Sport Teams, and developed the Fan Based Brand-Equity Model. They applied the Keller's (2003) Customer Based Brand Equity Pyramid Model (CBBE) and developed a Fan Based Brand-Equity Model. This model can be used to enhance the brand equity of the sporting event by enhancing the sporting event awareness, its imagery and performance, judgment of fans and their feelings and at the end develop and retain brand loyalty.

IPL the biggest international sporting event is considered to be one of the most successful at such a large-scale business model. It is interesting to know how players bidding happen and how franchises strategies to pick a player on the basis of his past performance in last season IPL and in other T-20 and other formats. Also how the star players or tem leaders can influence the performance of a franchise team, Bhattacharya, S. & Bhattacharya, S. (2012). IPL franchises strive for sustainable strategies but in the light of controversies and high cost revenue model and fluctuating

TRPs it has been a roller-costar ride for the franchise owners, Kadapa, S. S. (2013). Identifying ten key issues that has damaged the reputation of this sporting event, Kadapa, S. S. (2013), questions the past wrong doings of the IPL. These issues are:

1. The past saw many brands leaving IPL and IPL brand value falling
2. Can we repeat the success of IPL for other ports?
3. Big money the only attraction
4. Is it sustainable?
5. Is it profitable for franchises?
6. Is the franchise revenue model sustainable?
7. Has commercialization ruined the gentlemen sport?
8. Does "Cricket a game of chance" taken too seriously in its' management
9. Are media & sponsors getting their expected ROI?
10. How will these controversies impact the IPL Fan's perception?

Well, once and imperial game the power has now shifter to the sub-continent India, where BCCI has emerged as the richest and strongest cricketing governing body in the world. The game is highly commercialized and has become a business of commodities. The power structure of the world cricket has changed and has become completely opposite of what it use to be in the past (Gupta, A., 2017). Below is the process IPL:

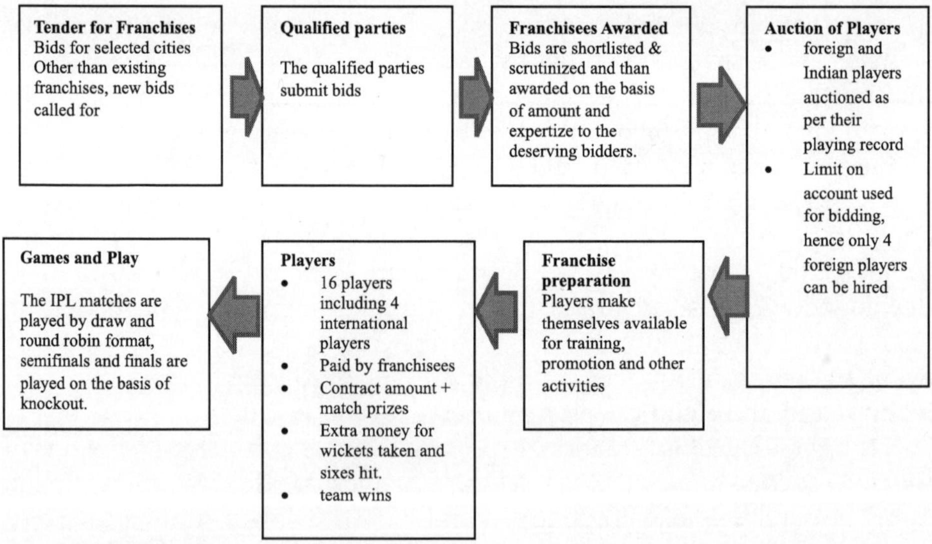

Figure 8: IPL Process

Source: Kapadia, Shashi (2013), "How sustainable is the strategy of the Indian Premier League - IPL? A critical review of 10 key issues that impact the IPL Strategy", International Journal of Scientific and Research Publications, Volume 3, Issue 12

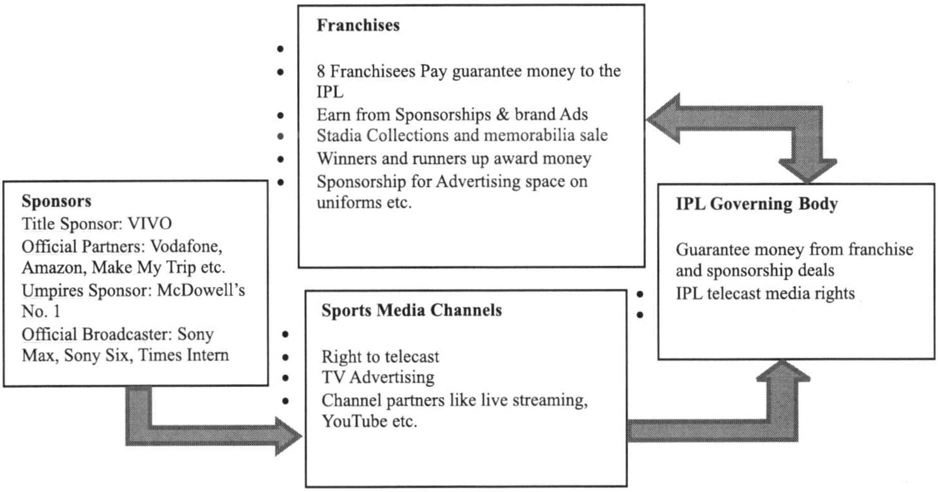

Figure 9: IPL Revenue Model - *a Big Money Spinner*

Source: Kapadia, Shashi (2013), "How sustainable is the strategy of the Indian Premier League - IPL? A critical review of 10 key issues that impact the IPL Strategy", International Journal of Scientific and Research Publications, Volume 3, Issue 12

Last 10 years of IPL has witnessed many fluctuations in the Brand Value of IPL. The brand Value of IPL has not been able to reach its' all time high of 4.1 $ Billion in last 7 years (Figure 9) due to many instances of controversial events and scandals.

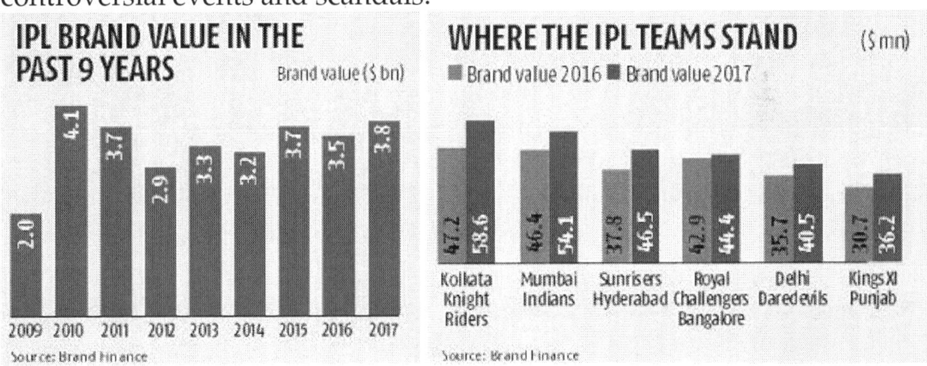

Fig. 10 *IPL Brand Value - From "IPL scores big on brand value", Business Standard (May 25th, 2017).*

After the 10th IPL, the franchises need to release their players and a fresh auction of the players will take place for the 2018 IPL tournament. The players are selected through the auction and hence it is easy to evaluate the brand value of the players (Parker, D., Burns, P., & Natarajan, H., 2008). Also their performance in IPL has been under scrutiny as it has been assumed that IPL is responsible for their global games performance (Saikia, H., Bhattacharjee, D., & Bhattacharjee, A., 2012).

GAP IN THE EXISTING LITERATURE

- The literature on Brand Doppelgänger has not discussed about the gaps between the theoretical knowledge of the subject matter and the actual measurement of the same in the brand front.
- The literature still leaves the Doppelgänger brand image as an ambiguous phenomenon and there have been no structured framework and models designed in the context of its measurement and impact.
- According to the existing literature the Doppelgänger brand image has been considered to be negative association but failed to measure its impact.
- The literature still assumes that the brand Doppelgänger image arouse from negative associations leading to brand avoidance and ignores the positive impact it may have on the brand health.
- A very limited literature could be found on the effect of brand Doppelgänger on the basis of its brand associations.

Figure 11

The literature review has covered the various components/dimensions of the brand doppelgänger image. We revisited the brand and branding phenomenon and how critical it is for any organization to have a strong brand. We also discussed how culture jamming is a creator of doppelgänger brand imagery and how offline and online consumer backlash can create monstrous doppelgänger imagery. Though we are able to establish the phenomenon of brand doppelgänger and how it can damage the brand but the literature on Brand Doppelgänger has not discussed about the gaps between the theoretical knowledge of the subject matter and the actual measurement of the same in the brand front.

The literature still leaves the Doppelgänger brand image as an ambiguous phenomenon and there have been no structured framework and models designed in the context of its measurement and impact. This makes the marketers jittery, as they don't know the gap between what they sell and how consumer consumes. They still operate on a customer complaint-feedback mold and do not understand the impact of this intangible monstrous imagery called the Doppelgänger brand.

According to the most of the existing literature the Doppelgänger brand image has been considered to be negative association but in some cases despite the Doppelgänger being strong it has actually helped the brand. Therefore, it is essential to understand the strength, weaknesses and the direction of this Doppelgänger imagery.

The literature still assumes that the brand Doppelgänger image arouse from negative associations leading to brand avoidance and ignores the positive impact it may have on the brand health.

A very limited literature could be found on the effect of brand Doppelgänger on the basis of its brand associations.

The varied categorization of doppelgänger elements itself has not been carried out in detail.

RATIONALE OF THE STUDY

- Empowered by Facebook, YouTube and other social media the consumers are delineating their own volition point of view/ perspective on brand messages based on the positive or negative association created in their mind. The brand Doppelgänger created through negative brand associations is of paramount interest to the marketers.
- Not only is the phenomenon worth researching but also measuring the impact of the Doppelgänger brand image will be of great importance to analytically ensure a brand's performance.
- This area of research has been selected taking into consideration the criticality of negative associations leading to brand Doppelgänger and its monstrous characteristics to destruct a brand. Therefore there was a need gap to empirically analyze how to manage brand performance.
- There's a tremendous need to empirically measure the impact of various influencers on a brand; this quantitative metric allows calibrated interventions.
- The before intervention and after intervention status of a brand can thus be quantitatively measured, allowing effectiveness and efficiency studies. As of now, only "creative feel" of the intervention and possible effect on topline are the sole measurement metrics.
- The monolithic nature of a brand can be splintered into network of influencers, the influencers can be labeled into positives and negatives, and the extent of positivity/ negativity can be ascertained with reasonable accuracy.
- The perceptions of Doppelgänger can be fixed as per assessing community of buyers, allowing brand custodians to prioritise target groups on the interventional campaigns; this shall also

allow supposedly confusing and paralyzing status of same influencer as positive or negative as per the community being contrasted.

- This shall open doors to applying the framework revealed here to other brands in the economy, and extend the work. This shall bringfroth control on brand's evolution for the custodians.
- The weight a community carries in the target universe can be correlated to the perceptional change/ delta so decided.
- The experts would get a reality check as they may have been incorrectly assessing a brand on idealism and philosophical parameters, unconnected with real world dynamics.
- A model was needed to periodically assess a brand's change in perception as per a creative campaign at its various points of life cycle.

❐

CHAPTER - THREE

RESEARCH METHODOLOGY

RESEARCH OBJECTIVES

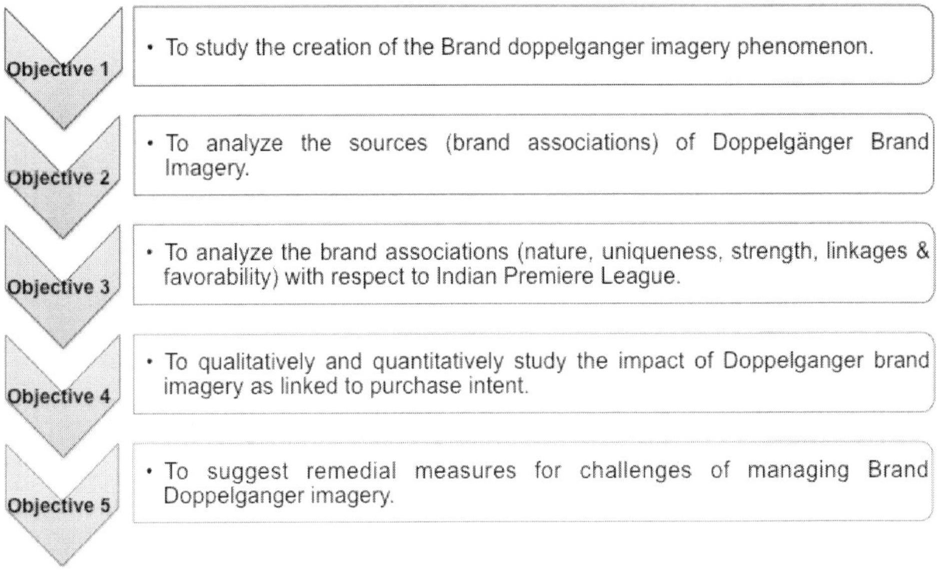

Figure 12

This study has primarily focussed upon the primary data sources collected from cricket experts and youngsters. The tool that was designed to collect the data was administered to the respondents across Delhi – NCR through personal interviews.

SIZE OF SAMPLE

Out of the initial population frame, 50 sports experts and 200 youngsters (students) were contacted across various Delhi/NCR universities out of which a filtered data of 35 experts and 156 students has been extracted up. The entire process of data collection took about 8 months starting from March 2016 to October 2016.

PROFILE OF RESPONDENTS

The study covers the respondents who were post-graduate students age 21-31. Both male and female respondents were considered for the collection of relevant information.

RESPONDENTS' DEMOGRAPHICS

Age Group	
21-31 yrs	100%
Gender	
Male	53.85%
Female	46.15%
Educational Qualification	
Graduation	100%
Level of Familiarity	
High	47.44%
Low	52.56%

Table 1

RESPONDENT SCREENING CRITERIA

The respondents who have given the data have been screened on the basis of screening question. Out of the total 200 respondents, only 156 could qualify the screening and 44 have been removed at the time of analysis. Further split into high and low familiarity was done.

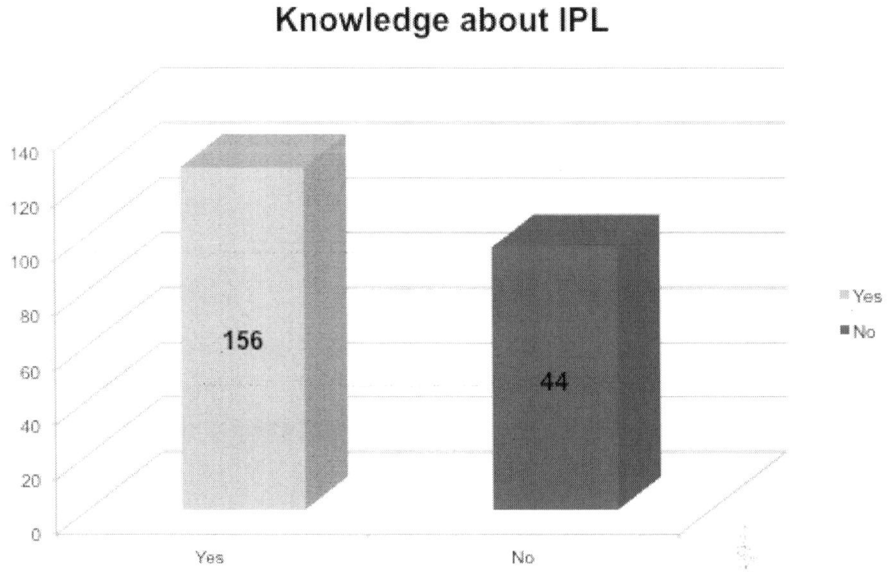

Figure 13

RESEARCH METHODOLOGY

There exist a host of consumer mapping techniques and analytical techniques that can be used for measuring impact of a brand, viz. (John, D.R., Loken, B., Kim, K., & Monga, A. B., 2006). Of these, Advanced Brand Concept Mapping, Schnittka, O., Sattler, H., & Zenker, S., (2012) belonging to the consumer mapping techniques family has been preferred for this research. Initially, it looked as if, the study should take recourse to application of the Zaltman Metaphor Elicitation Technique (ZMET) (Zaltman, Gerald, 1997). This was thought knowing that Brand Perceptions emanate from both conscious and unconscious seats of consumers. The founding assumption arises from Mehrabian's (1971) reporting that 93 percent of message is non-verbal. In case of Doppelgänger Brand Imagery, this becomes significant, as the consumers may not freely share their reasons for thinking negative. They may not freely reveal the impact of a particular Doppelgänger Brand Imagery on consumer perception of a brand. Further, it needs to be seen how these associations or linkages may lead to negative purchase behaviour. This research is better possible in Brand Concept Mapping (John, D.R., Loken, B., Kim, K., & Monga, A.B., 2006). Since the respondents are taken through a guided personal interview, the core beliefs are unearthed much more reliably than with other tools.

Now, brand image is read as strength, uniqueness and favourability of brand association, organized in a network (Keller, 2003). Brand Concept Mapping has been seen to just reveal two facets, viz. strength and uniqueness of the associations. It uncovers structural linkages of underlying brand associations – it even indicates strength of these linkages (Schnittka et al 2012). The psychoanalytic dimension thus gets due merit and attention.

However, Advanced Brand Concept Mapping (ABCM), Schnittka, O., Sattler, H., & Zenker, S., (2012) makes more sense, as it helps identify the third dimension, i.e. favourability through its metrics like Brand Association Network Value (BANV) (Schnittka, O., Sattler, H., & Zenker, S., 2012). For our study, favorability has to be deciphered as that is what helps segregate positive perceptions from negative ones, as Doppelgänger Brand Image demands. This is not merely qualitative; it in fact quantitative analysis of the brand association networks overall favorability by combining the uniqueness and strength of brand associations on one hand and the favorability of individual brand associations and the importance of that brand association to the buying decision of the consumer (Schnittka, O., Sattler, H., & Zenker, S., 2012).

Having decided to resort to ABCM, the plan is to take the study through the elicitation stage, targeting randomly identified respondents of various segments which hold a viewpoint about IPL (viewers; journalists & cricket experts; players & organizers; at least 30 in each category) and list various relevant brand associations and graph them as per the BCM model. As per ABCM approach we try to assess the validity (nomological & predictive) of the Brand associative network value; this is achieved by measuring the consumers' perception and attitude toward the brand, the level of familiarity with the brand, and their intent towards buying the brand. These mappings are done on a seven point Likert scale. Further we will apply a multinomial logit (MNL) model to guesstimate the probabilities of customers' preferences.

Then the mapping stage is applied to randomly selected respondents on these categories. This shall reveal favorability, strength and uniqueness of various associations.

This research shall uncover hitherto unstudied aspects of Doppelgänger image, esp. how it arises, and what are its influencers. It proffers an analytical look into relative potency of these influencers, and thus allows creation of a dashboard on which the brand manager/owner can tweak positive and negative influencers of varied strengths. This permits revitalizing the brand for gaining competitive advantage. It helps to manage the Doppelgänger image and/or strengthen it as per discretion of the brand manager/ owner. Future research would gain by this foray, and come forth with different domain studies to extend the application of the insights unearthed.

In order to understand the Doppelgänger brand imagery of a particular brand in question (in this case it is Indian Premier League -

IPL, we need to analyze the brand equity of IPL. To understand the brand equity which involves identifying the network of brand associations in the memory of the respondents. The respondents identify the network of strong, favorable and unique brand associations in their minds. To capture the brand associations we applied the Brand Concept Maps, John, D. R., Loken, B., Kim, K., & Monga, A. B., (2006), for eliciting brand association maps from the respondents. We than aggregated the individual maps and developed a consensus map which included the core brand associations pertaining to the IPL brand imagery. This map showed the associations, which are directly linked to the IPL brand or linked indirectly to the brand and the brand associations. Two studies were conducted to validate the Brand Concept Map Methodology with respect to the Indian Premier League.

We also made sure that the positive and negative user-generated content (UGC) on the internet and through various media sources like Newspapers, TV, Radio including Internet captures the brand associations that enhances or damages the brand reputation of IPL. Despite the lack of literature on the knowledge of the monstrous phenomenon, known as doppelgänger brand image (DBI). An attempt was made to define doppelgänger brand image as the negative associations at the brand equity level. Keller (1993) defines brand equity as the network of strong, favorable and unique brand associations in consumer's memory.

Consumers generally develop these associations weather positive or negative in their minds from their brand exposure or/and experience. This brand experience can be a collective interaction with the brand messages through various mediums or through the first hand experience with the brand. Consumers Internet 2.0 world is not a passive audience to the brand messages, they believe in a two-way communication with the brands. They are not shy of expressing their support or discontent towards a particular brand. These consumers than express their attitude towards the brand by posting their expressions on the social media platform (facebook, linkedin, twitter, youtube etc). These cultural backlashes is known as the "Doppelgänger Brand Imagery" – the negative consumer generated stories circulated on the internet through social media– (Thompson, C. J., Rindfleisch, A., & Arsel, Z., 2006). According to Earle (2002), "the central question about these brand parodies and social criticisms is whether they actually hurt a brand and whether a firm should take action to combat them." These viral culture-jamming phenomenon influences the brand associations in the consumer minds. Thompson, et al. argues that brands that follow emotional-branding strategies create opportunity for the emergence of a doppelgänger brand image and big brands are more vulnerable to a Doppelgänger Brand Imagery phenomenon.

In an ideal situation a company should measure these brand associations to develop a Brand Concept Map, not only to identify the brand associations but also to find out how these associations are linked to the brand and to one another. However there are not many methodologies to develop brand maps, though many methods are there for eliciting brand associations from consumers. These methods are qualitative like focus groups and quantitative such as attribute rating scales. But these techniques fail to identify brand associations and how they are linked to the brand, how one association is linked to another and how they are grouped together.

These techniques differ in the way they derive the brand maps. The first one was developed by Zaltman and Coulter (1995) known as the Zaltman's Metaphor Elicitation Technique (ZMET), this is a qualitative research technique which identifies key brand associations with in-depth interviews with the consumers and establishes links between these associations. The "analytical mapping" developed by Henderson, Iacobucci, and Calder (1998) is the second category of quantitative technique, producing brand maps using analytical method. They use consumer perceptions about a particular brand and develop brand association structure through network algorithms. Now both of these methods of developing brand network associations require experts from the various fields of psychology and neurosciences and also it is quite labor intensive. Whereas, the quantitative technique requires knowledge of statistical techniques, which may or may not be the core strength of the researcher.

Therefore this research has chosen the Brand Concept Mapping Technique - BCM, which is easy to apply and administer at the same time. BCM technique also provides evidence of its split-half validity and nomological reliability. We have divided this study into two parts:

1. Application of Brand concept maps in the context of the premier sports event – the Indian Premier League – IPL.
2. Application of the "Advance Brand Concept Maps" to evaluate the favorability of brand association networks in the context of IPL.

According to John et al. (2006) the Brand Concept Mapping – a methodology for identifying brand association networks comprises of three stages:

1. **Elicitation** Stage: wherein the brand associations are elicited from the consumers
2. **Mapping** Stage: wherein consumers map the elicitation to show how they are connected to the brand and to each other.
3. **Consensus mapping**: wherein the researcher develops a consensus brand map from the individual brand maps and associated data.

Zaltman's Metaphor Elicitation Technique– Zaltman and Coulter (1995) has described step by step these three stages in detail in order to understand consumer's thought about brands. The elicitation stage which involves small number of respondents (30-40) which uses photographs and images followed by a in depth personal interview to elicit construct. The interviews use qualitative techniques to capture verbal constructs such as Kelly's repertory grid and laddering exercises. This is followed by the mapping stage where the researcher reviews the individual constructs and ask the respondent to develop a map that shows the important connections among important constructs. The researcher than develops a consensus map in the aggregation stage in which the researcher reviews the important constructs and maps from the respondent's data to develop a consensus map that shows the important connections among important constructs. The researcher after reviewing decides on which construct or construct relationship are important to be included in the consensus map. The researcher here makes sure that he/she includes the most frequently mentioned constructs and develop a connect between the constructs to develop a consensus map.

Though the ZMET has its advantage, as it is a thorough technique to elicit brand associations but also employees various qualitative techniques to capture verbal and non-verbal consumer's expressions. Though ZMET establishes reliability and validity with the brand but validity between the associations is still an issue with the ZMET method. Despite ZMET's being a labor intensive and needs expert researchers, it also has a limited flexibility in constructing brand maps from the elicitation, mapping and aggregation stage as they are so intertwined.

BRAND CONCEPT MAP:

In order to understand the Doppelgänger brand imagery of a particular brand in question (in this case it is Indian Premier League - IPL, we need to analyze the brand equity of IPL. To understand the brand equity which involves identifying the network of brand associations in the memory of the respondents. The respondents identify the network of strong, favorable and unique brand associations in their minds. To capture the brand associations, we applied the Brand Concept Maps, John, D. R., Loken, B., Kim, K., & Monga, A. B. (2006), for eliciting brand association maps from the respondents. We then aggregated the individual maps and developed a consensus map, which included the core brand associations pertaining to the IPL brand imagery. These maps showed the associations, which are the core associations and are directly connected to the IPL brand, linked indirectly to the brand and the associations, which are grouped together. We then conducted two studies to establish reliability (consistency of measure) and validity (accuracy of the measure) of the Brand Concept Map Methodology with respect to the Indian Premier League.

We also made sure that the positive and negative user-generated content (UGC) on the internet and through various media sources like Newspapers, TV, Radio including Internet captures the brand associations that enhances or damages the brand reputation of IPL. Though there is a lack of literature on how to measure the value destruction, known as doppelgänger brand image (DBI). We tried to define doppelgänger brand image as the negative associations at the brand equity level. Keller (1993) defines brand equity as the network of strong, favorable and unique brand associations in consumer's memory.

Consumers generally develop these associations weather positive or negative in their minds from their brand exposure or/and experience. This brand experience can be a collective interaction with the brand messages through various mediums or through the first hand experience with the brand. Consumers Internet 2.0 world is not a passive audience to the brand messages, they believe in a two-way communication with the brands. They are not shy of expressing their support or discontent towards a particular brand. These consumers than express their attitude towards the brand by posting their expressions on the social media platform (facebook, linkedin, twitter, youtube etc). These cultural backlash is known as the "Doppelgänger Brand Imagery - that is, a family of disparaging images and stories about a brand that are circulated in popular culture by a loosely organized network of consumers, anti-brand activists, bloggers, and opinion leaders in the news and entertainment media" – Thompson, C. J., Rindfleisch, A., & Arsel, Z. (2006). According to Earle (2002), the central question about these brand parodies and social criticisms is whether they actually hurt a brand and whether a firm should take action to combat them. These viral culture-jamming phenomenon influences the brand associations in the consumer minds. Thompson, et al. argues that emotional-branding strategies are conducive to the emergence of a doppelgänger brand image and big brands are more vulnerable to a Doppelgänger Brand Imagery phenomenon.

In an ideal situation a company should measure these brand associations to develop a Brand Concept Map, not only to identify the brand associations but also to find out how these associations are linked to the brand and to one another. However there are not many methodologies to develop brand maps, though many methods are there for eliciting brand associations from consumers. These methods are qualitative like focus groups and quantitative such as attribute rating scales. But these techniques fail to identify brand associations and how they are linked to the brand, how one association is linked to another and how they are grouped together.

These techniques differ in the way they derive the brand maps. The first one was developed by Zaltman and Coulter (1995) known as the Zaltman's Metaphor Elicitation Technique (ZMET), this is a qualitative research technique which identifies key brand associations with in-depth interviews with the consumers and establishes links between these associations. The "analytical mapping" developed by Henderson, Iacobucci, and Calder (1998) is the second category of quantitative technique, producing brand maps using analytical method. They use consumer perceptions about a particular brand and develop brand association structure through network algorithms. Now both of these methods of developing brand network associations require experts from the various fields of psychology and neurosciences and also it is quite labor intensive. Whereas, the quantitative technique requires knowledge of statistical techniques, which may or may not be the core strength of the researcher.

Therefore this research has chosen the Brand Concept Mapping Technique - BCM, which is easy to apply and administer at the same time. BCM technique also provides evidence of its split-half validity and nomological reliability. We have divided this study into two parts:

3. Application of Brand concept maps in the context of the premier sports event – the Indian Premier League – IPL.
4. Application of the "Advance Brand Concept Maps" to evaluate the impact of brand association networks on the purchase intent (favorability) in the context of IPL.

According to John et al. (2006) there are three stages in the brand concept mapping for identifying brand association networks:

1. **Elicitation** Stage: wherein the brand associations are elicited from the consumers
2. **Mapping** Stage: wherein consumers map the elicitation to show how they are connected to the brand and to each other.
3. **Consensus mapping**: wherein the researcher develops a consensus brand map from the individual brand maps and associated data.

Zaltman's Metaphor Elicitation Technique – Zaltman and Coulter (1995) has described step by step these three stages in detail in order to understand consumer's thought about brands. The elicitation stage which involves small number of respondents (30-40) which uses photographs and images followed by a in depth personal interview to elicit construct. The interviews use qualitative techniques to capture verbal constructs such as Kelly's repertory grid and laddering exercises. This is followed by the mapping stage where the researcher reviews the individual constructs and ask the respondent to develop a map that shows the important connections among important constructs. The researcher than develops a consensus map in the aggregation stage in which the researcher reviews the important constructs and maps from the respondent's data to develop a consensus map that shows the important connections among important constructs. The researcher after reviewing decides on which construct or construct relationship are important to be included in the consensus map. The researcher here makes sure that he/she includes the most frequently mentioned constructs and develop a connect between the constructs to develop a consensus map.

Though the ZMET has its advantage, as it is a thorough technique to elicit brand associations but also employees various qualitative techniques to capture verbal and non-verbal consumer's expressions. Though ZMET establishes reliability and validity with the brand but validity between the associations is still an issue with the ZMET method. Despite ZMET's being a labor intensive and needs expert researchers, it also has a limited flexibility in constructing brand maps from the elicitation, mapping and aggregation stage as they are so intertwined.

❐

CHAPTER - FOUR

ANALYSIS & FINDINGS IPL'S BRAND CONCEPT MAPS

The application of concept maps is used for last twenty years in the field of physical sciences. The concept maps uses both structured and unstructured procedures to derive the concept maps from the consumers/ respondents. The unstructured concept maps required respondents to develop concept maps by mapping their set of brand associations for a chosen brand. Whereas in the structured procedure the respondents are aided with certain associations to develop a concept map based on the given brand associations. In BCM technique participant are given briefing on how to develop a concept map and then they are asked to think as to what comes in their mind when they think about the brand. The respondent then elicits these associations and a map is created that illustrates the core and non-core associations and their linkages (connection) to the brand and to one other.

The limitation which the concept maps have is that they do not have a procedure to develop a consensus map from individual maps. The unstructured concept maps have the same challenges as the ZMET. According to John, D. R., Loken, B., Kim, K., & Monga, A. B. (2006) the aggregation has to be kept in mind while designing the individual maps. Therefore the Brand Concept Mapping approach structures the consensus maps through elicitation, mapping and aggregation stages of BCM.

The Brand Concept Maps captures the core brand associations derived from the brand perception of consumers. The respondents are asked open ended question as to "what comes in your mind when you think about IPL?." Open-ended question allowed the respondents to think freely and can identify the association, which are important to them and are not aided by the researcher. This reduces the biasness due to researcher prompting the respondent. Than the most frequented brand associations are selected from the final set of responses. For our study we included responses on brand associations that was spelled out by at least 50% of the respondents. We also made sure that we retain the respondent's expression of association and not tinker with the original expression.

In the start of the mapping stage prompted to think of the brand associations that come to their mind. These associations than are mounted on plastic cards and shown to the respondent to chose from. We also made blank cards in case any association is left and the respondent might wants to add a new one. The respondent than was given the plastic cards of associations and were asked to build their own brand concept maps. Respondent chose the brand associations they had selected and connected them to the brand and to the other associations. They then drew single, double and triple line connectors to mark the connection strength between associations. Whereas in the aggregation stage the individual maps were combined based on a set of rule, which are the frequencies of associations mentioned to construct a consensus map. The consensus map showed the core and non-core brand associations and how they are connected to each other and the brand.

The advantage the BCM technique has over the earlier concept mapping techniques is adding structure to the elicitation, mapping and aggregation stages in order to facilitate administration and analysis. Prior consumer research in identifying brand associations can also be used in the elicitation stage in order to straight away move to the mapping and aggregation stage. BCM also helps in collecting larger samples as compared to ZMET as it is faster for the respondents to develop the concept maps. Also this increases the scope of collection of data from different geographies and market segments. BCM has disadvantages too. It needs more in depth probing, as there might be excessive associations and interconnections, which needs to be narrowed down by the researcher's intervention. Though the individual maps are more valid, the aggregation might induce some biasness and might adversely affect the validity and reliability for the BCM methodology.

PROCEDURE

The interviews were conducted face to face and the respondents were told that this is a part of academic project and they have been chosen to identify IPL's brand associations according to them. The respondents were encouraged to express their own opinions and open-ended questions like, "what comes to their mind when they think about IPL?" were asked. To aid the respondents they were shown the earlier selected 25 IPL associations mounted on laminated cards. They were asked to choose any of those cards and can also fill-in blank laminated cards if they have some additional brand associations.

The respondents were explained the whole purpose of the BCM and were shown some BCM samples of other brands like Sony and GAP. The sample BCM was shown to the respondents to describe the types of associations, which might be included, how they can be linked to the brand and one another. The respondents were further explained the significance of the single, double and triple lines that connected the associations. The respondents were explained that these lines indicated the strength of the associations with the brand and with other association. The single line signifies week association, whereas the triple line signifies strong association.

After this the respondents developed their brand concept maps for IPL. Respondents were given the laminated cards with the associations and were asked to plot them on a sheet of black chart paper and connect them with single, double or triple line. Lastly the respondents were asked to express their feelings towards IPL and rate them on a 10 point scale, where 1 is extremely negative and number 10 is extremely positive. This was marked on the brand map next to the IPL name. Respondents answered questions on their IPL experience and familiarity with the format, players, rules etc. On an average a respondent took 60-90 minutes to complete the brand concept maps.

In order to develop an IPL brand consensus map, the research followed a five-point process:

Step 1: The first step involved the identification of the IPL's core brand associations. The associations with at least 50% of mention in the maps were selected for the purpose. Also we included the borderline associations, which were mentioned in 45% to 49% of the individual brand maps, particularly where the interconnections were ≥ than the other associations, which are the core associations. As this validated the hypoBook that more the connectivity between associations and core associations signals the importance of the association to the network (John, D. R., Loken, B., Kim, K., & Monga, A.B., 2006). Applying these aggregation rules for BCM, we found 12 core associations for IPL brand.

Step II: In order to make the consensus map, we need to identify the core brand associations based on:

(a) The frequency of first-order mentions,

(b) The ratio of first-order mentions and

(c) The type of interconnections (single, double or triple line). Finally the associations selected were with ratio of first-order mentions to total mentions of at least 50%, with more subordinate and superordinate connections, as first-order associations. Applying these aggregation rules for BCM, we found six core associations for IPL brand.

AGGREGATION RULES FOR BCM		
lect core brand associations	Frequency of mention	**Select brand associations that are:** 1. Include on at least 50% of maps 2. Include on 45%-49% of maps if the number of connections for core associations identified previously
t first order brand associatio	**Frequency of first order mentior** Ratio of first order mention Type of interconnection	**Select core brand associations that are:** 1. Have a ratio of first order mentions to total mentions of atleast 50 2. Have more superordinates than subordinate interconnections
lect core brand associations	Frequencies for association links	**Select core brand association links by:** 1. Finding inflection pointon frequency plot 2. inflection point = target number 3. Including all association links that appear on or above the target n
non-core brand association l	Frequencies for association links	**Select non-core brand association links that are:** 1. Link to a core brand association 2. Linked on or above the target number of maps
ct number of connecting line	ean number of lines used per lin	**Select Single, Double, or Tripple lines for each brand association lin** 1. Determining the mean number of lines used per link 2. Rounding up or down to the next integer number (e.g. 2.3 = 2)

Table 2 – Aggregation Rules For BCM

Step III: Further we worked towards the remaining brand associations. We placed them on the consensus map, making sure that they are linked to if not all at least one of the first-order mentioned brand association. Since we need to place the links between the 12-core brand associations on the consensus map, therefore we analyzed link frequency between the specific associations placed on the maps. After combining the frequency count for different association links in different maps (figure 4), it was found that there were109 different links in only one respondents map, 42 different associations link appearing in two respondent maps and so on.

In order to find out that which are the links for associations that have to be incorporated in the consensus map we used these frequencies. As per the figure 4 the associations were plotted the inflection point at five, as the objective was to include all core associations linkages found in at least five individual maps. Though there were 22 links that met the criteria but only 12 of these links were associated with the brand associations that are core to the brand and the links beside the core were associated with the core and non-core associations or two or more non-core associations. Therefore we chose those core association links and placed them on the brand consensus map.

Step IV: In this step, the core and non-core brand association links were added to the consensus map. Though from a management perspective the core brand associations are the most important consideration set but the non-core associations are also important from customer's perception point of view as they influence the core associations and plays an important part in understanding the consumer's perception about the brand. To distinguish between the core and non-core association we represented the core association with the solid background and the non-core with the blank/white background.

Step V: In order to identify the strength of the connections between associations we used the single, double and triple lines and plotted them on the map. In order to figure out how many lines can be used on the consensus map, we computed the average number of lines for each association link the respondent used and rounded it to the nearest integer (e.g. 4.4 = 4).

IPL'S CONSENSUS BRAND CONCEPT MAP:

The IPL consensus brand concept map included both positive and negative brand associations, as IPL is a popular sports event and also is marked by controversies like fixing, betting, black money etc. The respondents were not only influenced by the IPL live matches updates, TV programming, star players but also had a negative influence from the negative publicity arising from the IPL controversies. Also most of the respondent were youth and therefore were active on the social media. They not only are the creator of Internet content but also get influenced by the user - generated content on IPL. IPL has a almost 58:42 as ratio of positive and negative sentiments (30db.com as on May 5th, 2016) floating on the internet particularly the social media like facebook, twitter, youtube etc.

AGGREGATION RULES FOR BCM:

We coded and tabulated the responses registered by each respondent's individual brand maps. We coded the following information:

All the 25 associations that occurred in the maps

The strength and linkages of each association to the brand or other associations.

The core and non-core associations (Core = connected to the brand, Non-core = connected to the core associations)

The position of these associations (above or below) on the brand concept map.

Additional associations added by the respondents beside the 25 initial associations were analyzed based on its frequency and determine whether any associations were mentioned enough time to be added to the original set of associations.

The additional mentioned association were mentioned by not more than 7% of the respondents, so they were excluded from the final set of associations

BCM Measures for IPL Fans							
	Core Associations			First order associations			
A	B	C	D	E	F = E/C*100	G	H
S.No.	Brand associations	Frequency of mention	umber of Interconnection	Frequency of first order mention	Ratio of first order mention (%)	Subordinate connections	Superordinate connections
1	Cricket	141	167	83	58.9	58	109
3	20-20	126	138	53	42.1	73	65
5	Entertainment	116	131	98	84.5	18	113
21	Star owners	115	126	88	76.5	27	99
2	High Paced	111	90	51	45.9	60	30
7	Auction	121	121	72	59.5	49	72
24	Conflict of interest	107	164	60	56.1	47	117
17	Betting	106	134	55	51.9	51	83
23	Contests	105	111	48	45.7	57	54
20	Black Money	100	140	77	77.0	23	117
4	Franchise	100	122	42	42.0	58	64
11	Parties	100	86	35	35.0	65	21
8	Glamour	96	129	44	45.8	52	77
12	Global Level	96	66	31	32.3	65	1
15	Format	88	109	35	39.8	53	56
16	High Profile	84	96	24	28.6	60	36
18	Overdose of cricket	81	55	43	53.1	38	17
22	International Players	61	70	42	68.9	19	51
9	Controversial	58	32	27	46.6	31	1
25	Music	55	43	32	58.2	23	20
10	Fixing	29	38	14	48.3	15	23
14	Not a gentlemen sport	14	17	3	21.4	11	6
6	Cheer Girls	9	16	5	55.6	4	12
19	BCCI	5	9	3	60.0	2	7
13	Players' Conflict	5	4	3	60.0	2	2

Table 3 – BCM Measure for IPL Fans

BCM MEASURES FOR IPL FANS

Frequency of Mention: The number of times a brand association is mentioned across all the individual maps.

Number of Interconnections: How many times that a brand association is connected to other brand association. For example in Table 4. "Cricket" was the most frequently mentioned brand association, therefore, "Cricket" with many interconnections becomes the "CORE" brand association on the consensus brand map.

Frequency of first order mention: It is the measure of the number of times that a brand association is directly linked to the brand across all individual maps. For example in Table 1. "20 – 20" was the most frequently and directly connected to the IPL brand.

Ratio of first order mention: When a brand association is included on a brand map, it is the percentage of time that it is linked directly to the brand. For example in Table 1. "Entertainment" was included and directly linked to the IPL brand by 84.6% of respondents on their brand maps.

Subordinate & Superordinate Connections: They are the types of interconnections, which indicate the frequency of placement of the brand association above other associations (Subordinate) or below other associations (Superordinate). For example "High Paced Game" frequently mentioned brand association was placed at the subordinate position in 60 maps and at superordinate position in 30 maps. Therefore, the association with more subordinate than superordinate connections has a high chance for being connected directly to the IPL brand.

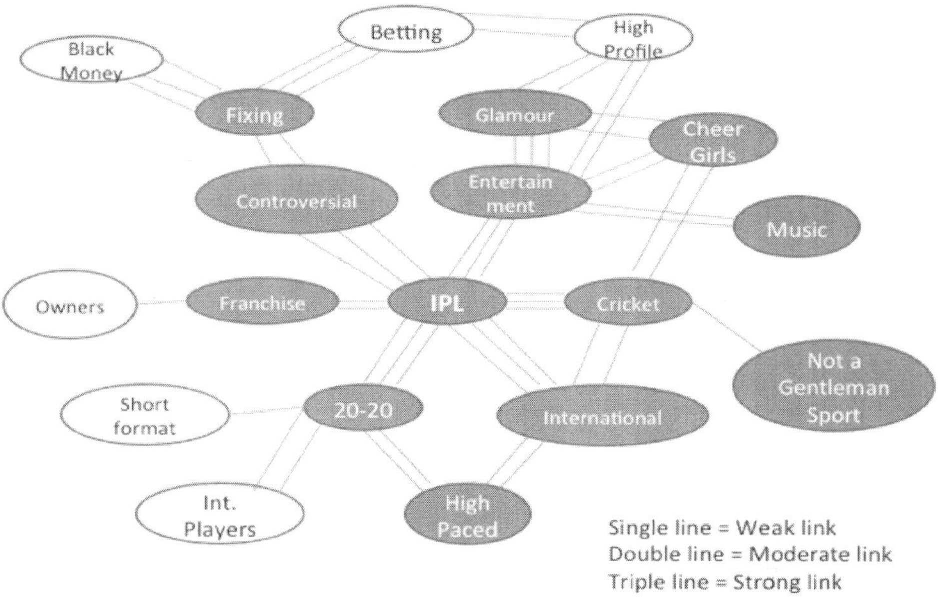

Figure 14 - IPL's Consensus Brand Concept Map

RELIABILITY AND VALIDITY TESTS

After applying the brand concept map method and capturing the brand associations through consumers' perception about the Indian Premiere League and plotting them in a network of associations, we need to assess the reliability and validity of our analysis. In order to test the consistency of our analysis in drawing out the IPL's consensus brand concept map we conducted the split-half reliability test We divided the consumer sample into two equal halves and compared the findings of split-half I with the Split-half II, so as, we can measure the consistency of contribution of all parts of the test to what is being measured. Further, we conducted the nomological validity test by drawing a comparison between the familiar and not so familiar group (expert-novice test analysis). This was an important analysis, as we wanted to capture the knowledge structures of both experts and novice groups for IPL, and examine the difference between the two (if any). This will ensure that the brand concept method we applied measures what it claims to measure. The steps we followed were:

- Nomological validity was assessed through known-group approach, where consensus maps were arrived at between the familiar with IPL and not so familiar with IPL League.
- Because experts of the game tend to be more familiar, therefore, we expected to find many expert–novice differences while doing the comparison.

- After comparison it was found that the structure of the map for the respondents who were very familiar with IPL was more complex, where there were a thick network of associations.
- The respondents were divided into two groups: ***highly familiar*** and not so ***familiar***.
- Two kinds of analysis were conducted in order to assess if the BCM was capable of picking up expert–novice differences.
- Firstly, a consensus brand map was produced through aggregation principle for both familiarity and non-familiarity groups.
- The second analysis was conducted to determine the corroboration of these findings with individual BCM analysis.
- Thereafter BANV hierarchical values were arrayed and validated, this being the latest and best-advised brand mapping method. However, no study hitherto had ever applied this to Doppelgänger Imagery elements.
- Through the application of BCM, we could only assess the strength and uniqueness of brand associations, but not favorability.
- Further to quantify the favorability (purchase intent) of single brand associations and to quantify the overall network favorability we applied empirical application of the brand association network value (BANV).
- The research included an additional stage of evaluation as a part of the mapping of the associative network:
    1. An evaluative judgments of Consumers' on each brand association
    2. Each brand association's importance in consumer's purchase situation.

RELIABILITY ANALYSIS

Though the Brand Concept Map method captures the IPL's brand association network based on the perception of IPL's customers but does it pass the reliability & validity test of measurement? Also since are audience is divided equally into experts and non-experts of the age group 20-22 years and differ in their experience and perceptions with respect to the Indian Premier League. Therefore, we wanted to test the consistency of the brand concept maps across both the demographically and psychographically different segments of our respondents. Therefore Split-Half reliability test was applied to determine the consistency in the consensus maps across two completely different sets of respondents. According to the books, the Split-Half Reliability is defined as "a measure of reliability in which a test is split into two parts and an individual›s scores on both halves are compared." We checked the nomological validity by comparing the consensus maps from highly familiar groups and not so familiar group in order to determine the expert-novice differences between the two groups.

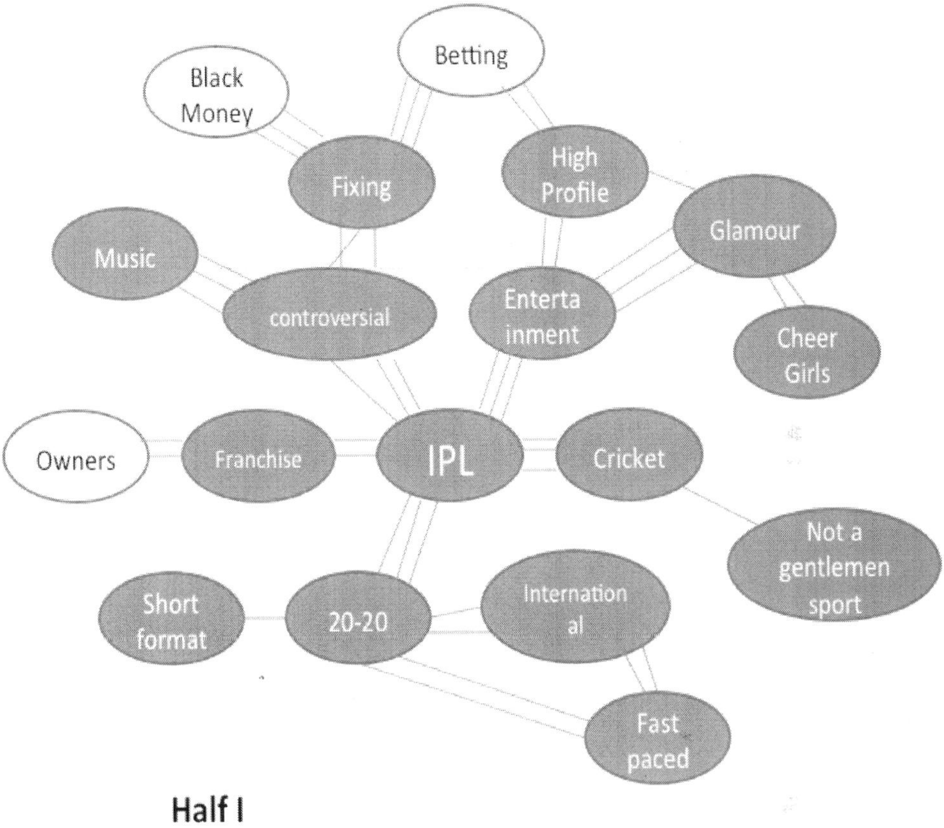

Figure 15 – BCM - Split Half I

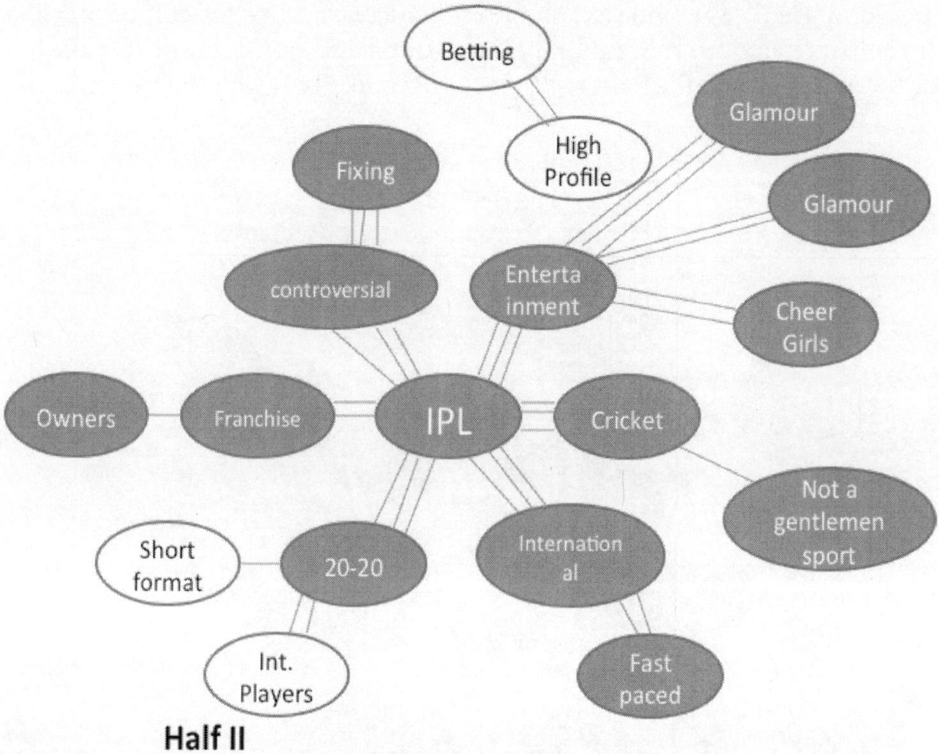

Figure 16 – Split Half II

SPLIT-HALF RELIABILITY

After applying the split-half reliability test on the Split-half I and Split-half II groups consensus maps were developed from their individual maps and after comparing the two as seen in figure 8 & 9, it was observed a reasonable degree of consistency. It was observed that both the maps have commonality of exactly similar first-order associations, with similarity in linkages through connected lines and many of the links between the associations were the same. The only exception was that the association "Franchises" was connected with a double line as compared to the other core associations, which were connected with the triple line. Also, the association "International Event" was an additional association.

In order to quantify the split-half reliability measures we followed the following steps:

(Analysis I):

We coded each split-half map for the presence or absence of

- Each of the 25 associations as core associations
- Each of the 25 brand associations as a first-order association
- Each of the 300 possible link among the 25 brand associations

↓

We coded presence of a brand association or association link as 1, and 0

↓

Conducted correlation across the split-half maps:

- Core brand associations (Highest) – $\Phi = .92$, $p < .01$; N = 25
- First-order brand associations (Moderately high) - $\Phi = .78$, $p < .01$; N = 25
- Brand association links (moderate) - $\Phi = .50$, $p < .01$; N = 300

Figure 17 – Split Half Reliability Test

Analysis II: The second analysis was conducted to gather data to conduct the reliability of the brand association linkages. Applying correlations between the two split halves and the consensus map, for the presence of association links the coefficient alpha is of .70 and for the strength of the association link the coefficient alpha is of .78, which both meets the acceptable level of reliability.

We coded each split-half map for the presence or absence of each of the 78 possible links between the 12 core beliefs of IPL

↓

We coded presence of a brand association or association link as 1, and 0

↓

Conducted correlation across each split-half maps:

- Core brand associations (moderately high) – $\Phi = .75$, $p < .01$; N = 78
- First-order brand associations (Moderately high) - $\Phi = .78$, $p < .01$; N=78
- Correlation between split-halves (moderate) - $\Phi = .54$, $p < .01$; N = 78

↓

Strength of the association links (single, double and triple lines) between all 78 possible links:

- Consensus and split-half I map – ($r = .75$, $p < .01$; N = 78)
- Consensus and split-half II map – ($r = .84$, $p < .01$; N = 78)
- And both split-half maps – ($r = .64$, $p < .01$; N = 78)

Figure 18 – Split Half Reliability (Strength)

THE BRAND ASSOCIATION NETWORK VALUE (BANV)

In order to capture the impact of the Doppelgänger brand imagery on the IPL brand, we followed the "Advance brand concept maps: a new approach for evaluating the favorability of brand association networks" – (Schnittka, O., Sattler, H., & Zenker, S., (2012). The advance concept maps extends the original brand concept map approach by measuring the favorability of an individual association and quantifies network of association's favorability. Therefore by applying the advance brand concept map approach we tend to compare the favorability of the individual brand association and favorability of the aggregate network of brand associations. As we have seen in the case of the IPL brand concept map that the respondents identified various brand associations both positive and negative related to IPL as per their knowledge and experiences. The respondents developed the IPL brand concept maps by constructing their own network of associations related to IPL. We then aggregated the information and developed a consensus brand concept map for IPL. The IPL brand concept maps then where subject to empirical study test for the reliability and therein validity of the brand concept map technique. The BCM technique elicits relevant brand associations, structure these associations in a network and assumes that these associations are unique to the brand in comparison with competition. Further it identifies the associations, which are core associations and are directly linked to the brand and with other associations by single (weak), double (moderate) and triple (strong) lines. But fails to provide explicit favorability information. Now according to Keller (1993) the favorability of brand association is a result of an individual evaluative judgment and according to Fishbein & Ajzen (1975) influences the overall purchase decision.

Because the study I, which develops a consensus brand concept map for IPL does not measure the favorability of brand associations, also does not give us any clue as to the favorability of the underlying association network. Therefore, we applied the advance concept map technique and its brand association network value (BANV) metric, as to measure the overall favorability of brand association networks by clubbing the uniqueness and strength with the favorability of single brand associations. In study I we followed the original BCM approach, which included three stages:

a) Through the first *Elicitation* stage the respondents identified the most important associations related to the IPL brand,

b) Through the Mapping stage the respondent developed brand concept map through network of IPL's brand associations and drawing linkages to the IPL brand and their connection to each other.

c) The third is the aggregation stage; the consensus map is developed, which makes sure that all of the selected brand associations are plotted on the brand concept map. The appearance of individual brand association plotted on the brand concept map has been classified as the - first-order association, which is the core association and is directly linked to the IPL brand, second order association, which are linked to the first-order association, and the strength of linkage (weak links = single lines, moderate links = double lines, and strong links = triple lines) connecting an association to the brand or to another association. Therefore in the consensus map for IPL we see that the solid circles are the core associations (occurring on at least 50% of the brand maps) and the blank circles are the non-core associations (occurring on less than 50% of the brand maps).

The IPL aggregation map in study I show the network structure and the nature of single brand association within the network for example IPL has six first order associations directly linked to the brand IPL. The consensus map also show the strength of the brand association connection – with the brand and with other associations through single, double or triple lines. For example we see that Cricket, Entertainment, International Event, 20-20 and Controversial are connected by triple lines and have the strongest linkages with the core brand IPL than the franchise association which is connected to the core brand with only the double line. Since the brand concept mapping technique does not provide any clue on the purchase intent of the single brand associations, therefore we applied an additional evaluation stage by including the evaluative judgments of consumers and the influence it has on consumer's buying decision.

In order to analyze the favorability of each association on consumers' brand purchase decision, we measured each brand association on a seven-point likert scale for positive and negative favorability (i.e., 1 = extremely high favorability; 7 = extremely low favorability). Likert Scale is named after an American psychologist Rensis Likert. "It is a psychological measurement device that is used to gauge attitudes, values, and opinions". In the Likert scale the respondents are suppose to indicate their agreement or disagreement to a series of statements in a questionnaire. A likert scale can range from a 5-point scale to a 10-point scale.

According to Keller (1993), all brand associations are not relevant in terms of importance for making a purchase decision, for example "Controversial" brand association though strongly linked to the IPL brand but the respondent rates the importance of it lesser than the brand associations like "Cricket" or "Entertainment". Well the study I might include the importance of each association by the strength of its linkages to the core brand and number if interconnections with the other associations. However, it does not explain the weightage of each brand association in the respondent's purchase decision. But for the IPL management it is important to know that which associations are affecting the brand IPL. Therefore, as a researcher it is utmost important for us to study the favorability of each association and its impact on the purchase decision or brand avoidance by the customers.

- Brand association network value (BANV), measures the favorability of brand association networks.
- Based on the multi-attribute attitude model, BANV measurement formula was developed by Fishbein and Ajzen (1975).
- Brand attitudes are the cognitive beliefs developed by consumers towards the brand.

$$\sum_{a=1}^{m} Eaj * Saj * Iaj * Laj$$

Eaj is the consumers' j's judgment of the brand association on a seven-point Likert scale. **(4 = neutral, 4+ = Positive & -4 = Doppelgänger)**

Saj represents the weak, moderate, or strong association s strength direct connection to its superordinate associations within the network or the core brand, stronger the linkages greater is the association impact on the BANV.

Iaj is the individual importance of that brand association to the buying decision

Laj is the position or level of placement of association Eaj on the network of associations.

All of these were to range on 7 point scales, with 1 as least value and 7 as most powerful, whilst 4 was a neutral middle ground.

Of course this entire research has been focused upon studying the Doppelgänger effect in brand analysis, with specific focus on IPL. This indeed needed an empirical analysis, with a possible quantitative calibration and measurement.

But what started as an intriguing thing, that Vardoulakis (2006) had given a brave contra-rendition, in delinking Doppelgänger with demonic, in fact showing it as having a potential of positivity, has been the climax of this study. In fact, the research brings a challenge to those who sit in silos, or in ivory towers, and pronounce judgments upon a brand.

These experts, no doubt having the best of interest of a brand in mind, and being endowed with experience and wisdom, do possess a deeper insight into what makes a brand. Having studied brands for decades, they have a better overview.

But all said and done, they are experts, and not the consumers or customers. A business depends on carving a share from wallet of customer. Thereby, the drivers of consumer behavior and customers' purchase dynamics are more vital. Topline and Bottomline are essential elements of judging a brand's business health.

This research has revealed what actually influences a customer to buy, which aspect he says as positive, which aspects he says as negative. How he composites an image in his mind to bring about a net buy or a net reject decision.

Further, beyond a lone customer, aggregation of customers on psychographic or geographical basis permits knowing what drivers move the aggregation prima facie. In fact why prim facie, but even at deeper level of cognitive decision-making.

This research is extremely useful in that sense.

With this introductory note, let us delve into detailed analysis of this unique kind of a research, never before attempted elsewhere.

Herein, findings after rigorous analysis of the data are presented. Collection and analysis of the data in response to the problems posed in initial stages of the research. There were two critical goals that drove the collection of the data and the subsequent analysis of the same. Those goals were to develop a base of knowledge about the doppelgänger impact as it is perceived and utilized relative to brand management. The other goal was to evolve calibration on quantitative grounds for various influencers. A tertiary goal that emanated was to determine if current perception and utilization of experts is consistent with the drivers perceived by a target group/ community. This went beyond scope of studying only intellectually, but also empirically.

These objectives were accomplished.

The findings presented in this chapter demonstrate the potential for merging theory and practice. Carefully analyzed and segregated tables and graphs have been laid down for easily deciphering what transpired. This has permitted giving salience to insights that were lurking beneath the morass of numbers.

RESPONDENTS & CATEGORIES

From 50 sports experts, 35 were narrowed down to benchmark the whole study. Of 200 students/ youth, 156 were zeroed in as respondents mapped against the experts. A total of 9 target groups/ communities were thus studied:

1. 84 Males,
2. 72 Females,
3. 74, High Familiarity youth,

4. 82 Low Familiarity youth,
5. 40 Males who were High Familiarity.
6. and 34 Females who were aloe High Familiarity,
7. 44 Males who were Low Familiarity,
8. and 38 Females who were also Low Familiarity,
9. and finally 156 Overall community.

Respondents

	Familiarity High	Familiarity Low	Total
Males	40	44	84
Females	34	38	72
Total	74	82	156

	Familiarity High	Familiarity Low	Total
Males	25.64%	28.21%	53.85%
Females	21.79%	24.36%	46.15%
Total	47.44%	52.56%	100.00%

Table 4: Respondents' vs Experts

A balanced yet heterogeneous group allowed multiple comparisons and permitted escaping biases a particular segment might have had.

CONSENSUS BCM FOR FAMILIARITY GROUP

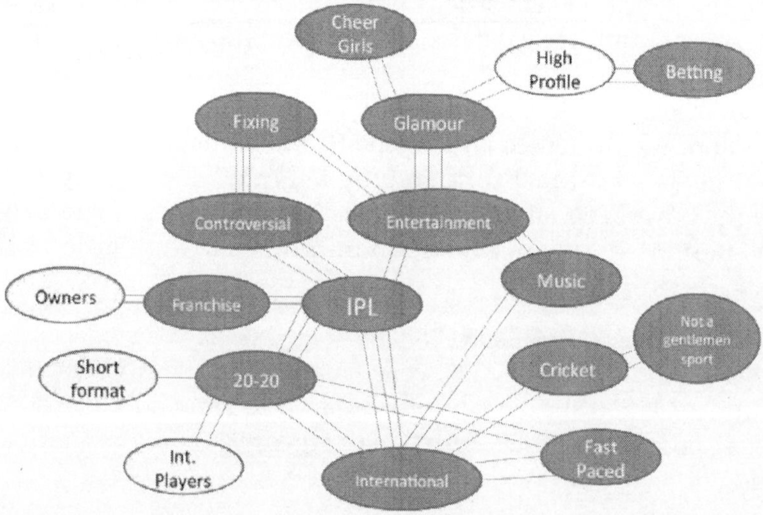

Very Familiar

Figure 19

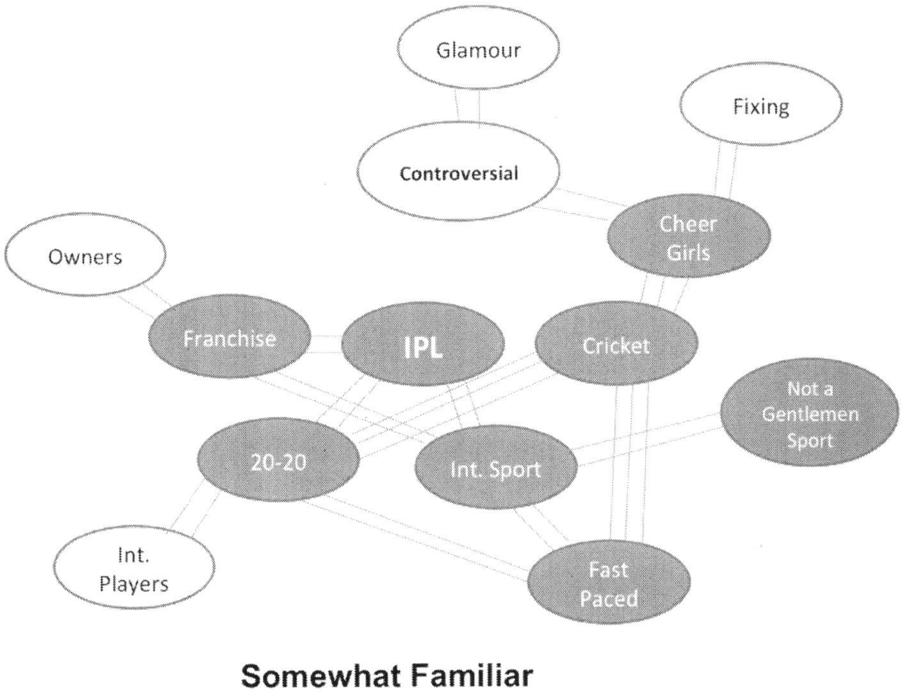

Figure 20 Consensus BCM for somewhat familiarity group

A variance analyses found out the structure of the brand concept maps of the familiar group and discovered that their brand maps are more complex and included more number of brand associations, many brand association links, had strong brand association links (triple lines), and hierarchy of branches with more third-level links.

CONSONANCE WITH EXPERTS

Every segment/ category. / community by itself and combinational with related segment was reckoned against the experts' labeling of the 25 elements. This pitching forth brought in contrasts and the self-revealing nature of calibrated degree of impact by influencers was analyzed threadbare. Within this, a composite index too was evolved that can become a gold standard on how exactly to analyze a brand on its influencers, not only as vanilla influencers, but also as labeled under Doppelgänger or not.

Interestingly, this also allowed separating the positive influencers into seen positive or negative by the target segment.

Further, it also permitted separately analyzing the Doppelgänger influencers into seen so or seen positively by the target segment.

The Experts had as per their discretion and best judgment tagged the elements as:

- Positive Influencers nee PI and
- Doppelgänger Influencers nee DI

In comparison, 4 options generated; a segment had:

- same positive influencer nee SPI
- flipped positive influencer nee FPI, making it in effect a Doppelgänger
- unchanged Doppelgänger influencer nee UDI
- reversed Doppelgänger influencer nee RDI, in effect making it a positive influencer

Item Code	Entity	Experts	Males High	Males Low	Females High	Females Low
1	Cricket	PI	SPI	SPI	SPI	SPI
2	High Paced	PI	SPI	SPI	SPI	SPI
3	20-20	PI	SPI	SPI	SPI	SPI
4	Franchise	PI	SPI	SPI	SPI	SPI
5	Entertainment	PI	SPI	SPI	SPI	SPI
7	Auction	PI	SPI	SPI	FPI	FPI
8	Glamour	PI	SPI	SPI	SPI	FPI
12	International/Global	PI	FPI	FPI	SPI	FPI
16	High Profile	PI	FPI	SPI	SPI	FPI
15	Format	PI	SPI	SPI	FPI	FPI
21	Star owners	PI	SPI	SPI	SPI	SPI
23	Contests	PI	SPI	FPI	FPI	FPI
22	International Players	PI	SPI	SPI	SPI	SPI
25	Music	PI	FPI	SPI	FPI	SPI
10	Fixing	DI	UDI	RDI	UDI	RDI
9	Controversial	DI	RDI	RDI	UDI	RDI
13	Players' Conflict	DI	RDI	RDI	UDI	RDI
6	Cheer Girls	DI	RDI	RDI	UDI	RDI
11	Parties	DI	RDI	RDI	RDI	RDI
14	Not a gentlemen sport	DI	UDI	UDI	UDI	RDI
19	BCCI	DI	UDI	UDI	RDI	UDI
18	Overdose of cricket	DI	UDI	RDI	RDI	RDI
20	Black Money	DI	UDI	UDI	UDI	UDI
17	Betting	DI	UDI	UDI	UDI	UDI
24	Conflict of interest	DI	UDI	RDI	RDI	RDI

Table 5: Doppelgänger influencer

Item Code	Entity	Label	Males Overall	Females Overall	High Familiarity Overall	Low Familiarity Overall	Overall
1	Cricket	PI	SPI	SPI	SPI	SPI	SPI
2	High Paced	PI	SPI	SPI	SPI	SPI	SPI
3	20-20	PI	SPI	SPI	SPI	SPI	SPI
4	Franchise	PI	SPI	SPI	SPI	SPI	SPI
5	Entertainment	PI	SPI	SPI	SPI	SPI	SPI
7	Auction	PI	SPI	FPI	SPI	FPI	FPI
8	Glamour	PI	SPI	SPI	SPI	SPI	SPI
12	Global Level	PI	FPI	FPI	FPI	FPI	FPI
16	High Profile	PI	FPI	SPI	FPI	FPI	FPI
15	Format	PI	SPI	FPI	SPI	SPI	SPI
21	Star owners	PI	SPI	SPI	SPI	SPI	SPI
23	Contests	PI	SPI	FPI	SPI	FPI	SPI
22	ernational Playe	PI	SPI	SPI	SPI	SPI	SPI
25	Music	PI	SPI	SPI	FPI	SPI	SPI
10	Fixing	DI	UDI	UDI	UDI	RDI	UDI
9	Controversial	DI	RDI	RDI	RDI	RDI	RDI
13	Players' Conflict	DI	RDI	UDI	RDI	RDI	RDI
6	Cheer Girls	DI	RDI	UDI	RDI	RDI	RDI
11	Parties	DI	RDI	RDI	RDI	RDI	RDI
14	a gentlemen sp	DI	UDI	UDI	UDI	RDI	UDI
19	BCCI	DI	UDI	UDI	UDI	UDI	UDI
18	verdose of crick	DI	UDI	RDI	RDI	RDI	RDI
20	Black Money	DI	UDI	UDI	UDI	UDI	UDI
17	Betting	DI	UDI	UDI	UDI	UDI	UDI
24	onflict of intere	DI	UDI	RDI	UDI	RDI	UDI

Table 6: Doppelgänger influencer (Male/female/familiarity)

DETAILED SEGMENT COMPARISONS WITH THE EXPERTS:

To be able to arrive at numeric equivalents of BANV for a category of customers is a tremendous stride. In a world of subjective commenting, to be able to have a number stand for the value it purports to measure is a revolution.

The precise measurement immediately allows comparisons of even apples and oranges. It further gives a basis for splitting advertising budgets on the basis of the BANVs it intends to correct, and by how much. Although the process of determining BANVs is elaborate and complex, but once done, it can be replicated.

This valid process is easily runnable in repeat iterations, without losing its sanctity.

Herewith the Eight segments have been individually analyzed in detail.

1. Males High versus the Experts:

Item Code	Entity	Expert	Males High
1	Cricket	PI	SPI
2	High Paced	PI	SPI
3	20-20	PI	SPI
4	Franchise	PI	SPI
5	Entertainment	PI	SPI
7	Auction	PI	SPI
8	Glamour	PI	SPI
12	Global Level	PI	FPI
16	High Profile	PI	FPI
15	Format	PI	SPI
21	Star owners	PI	SPI
23	Contests	PI	SPI
22	International Players	PI	SPI
25	Music	PI	FPI
10	Fixing	DI	UDI
9	Controversial	DI	RDI
13	Players' Conflict	DI	RDI
6	Cheer Girls	DI	RDI
11	Parties	DI	RDI
14	Not a gentlemen sport	DI	UDI
19	BCCI	DI	UDI
18	Overdose of cricket	DI	UDI
20	Black Money	DI	UDI
17	Betting	DI	UDI
24	Conflict of interest	DI	UDI

Table 7: Males High versus the Experts I

Same Positive Influencers were 11; Ironically, Flip Positive Influencers were 3;

The similar perception on influencers, which were Doppelgänger, was on 7; Whereas Reversal of Doppelgänger Influencers was on 4. This shows an overlap of Positive Influencers to the extent of 78.5% (a high). But the overlap on doppelgänger Influencers is only 63.63%

On an advanced level, the combined ESIL ratings are more revealing as they incorporate criticality in BANV maps.

		Experts	Males High	
Positive Influencers				**Beta**
	Same SPI	623.793	482.215	0.773
	Flip FPI	199.22	114.85	0.576
	Overall	510.793	438.663	0.859
Doppelgangers				
	Unchanged UDI	132.004	148.213	1.123
	Reversed RDI	200.043	318.897	1.594
	Overall	152.169	138.204	0.908
Overall		245.608	207.917	0.847

Table 8: Males High versus the Experts II

*Beta is the ratio of category ESIL per influencer to the same for Experts. A low beta means very different perception; a high beta implicates commonality of perception.

#Again an Overall low beta implies that segment views the brand as very weak compared to the Experts judgment, esp. as the negativity of Effective doppelgängers (UDI and FPI) is applied.

Notable here is, the target category tends to underplay the SPIs by 22.7%.

- The FPIs have got a big drubbing of 42.4%.
- The UDIs have experienced a reversal, exaggerating by 12.3%
- The reversed RDIs have gone through a massive 59.4% inflation.
- This depicts the gross error a brand custodian may have committed by moving on perception of Experts.

(2) Males Low versus Experts:

Item Code	Entity	Expert	Males Low
1	Cricket	PI	SPI
2	High Paced	PI	SPI
3	20-20	PI	SPI
4	Franchise	PI	SPI
5	Entertainment	PI	SPI
7	Auction	PI	SPI
8	Glamour	PI	SPI
12	Global Level	PI	FPI
16	High Profile	PI	SPI
15	Format	PI	SPI
21	Star owners	PI	SPI
23	Contests	PI	FPI
22	International Players	PI	SPI
25	Music	PI	SPI
10	Fixing	DI	RDI
9	Controversial	DI	RDI
13	Players' Conflict	DI	RDI
6	Cheer Girls	DI	RDI
11	Parties	DI	RDI
14	Not a gentlemen sport	DI	UDI
19	BCCI	DI	UDI
18	Overdose of cricket	DI	RDI
20	Black Money	DI	UDI
17	Betting	DI	UDI
24	Conflict of interest	DI	RDI

Table 9: Males Low versus Experts I

Same Positive Influencers were 12; Ironically, Flip Positive Influencers were 2;

The similar perception on influencers, which were Doppelgänger, was on only 4;

Whereas Reversal of Doppelgänger Influencers was on 7. This shows an overlap of Positive Influencers to the extent of 85.7% (very high). But the overlap on Doppelgänger Influencers is only 36.3% (very low)

On an advanced level, the combined ESIL ratings are more revealing as they incorporate criticality in BANV maps.

		Experts	Males Low	
Positive Influencers				Beta
	Same SPI	589.761	466.72	0.791
	Flip FPI	191.127	65.737	0.344
	Overall	440.002	387.741	0.881
Doppelgangers				
	Unchanged UDI	110.322	117.999	1.07
	Reversed RDI	183.273	252.347	1.377
	Overall	137.257	100.579	0.733
Overall		301.46	270.544	0.897

Table X: Males Low versus Experts II

*Beta is the ratio of category ESIL per influencer to the same for Experts. A low beta means very different perception; a high beta implicates commonality of perception.

#Again an Overall low beta implies that segment views the brand as very weak compared to the Experts judgment, esp. as the negativity of Effective doppelgängers (UDI and FPI) is applied.

Notable here is, the target category tends to underplay the SPIs by 20.9%.

- The FPIs have got a big drubbing of 65.6%.
- The UDIs have experienced a reversal, exaggerating by only 7%.
- The reversed RDIs have gone through a large 37.7% inflation.
- This depicts the erroneous picture a brand custodian may have committed by moving on perception of Experts.

(3) Females High Versus Experts:

Item Code	Entity	Expert	Females High
1	Cricket	PI	SPI
2	High Paced	PI	SPI
3	20-20	PI	SPI
4	Franchise	PI	SPI
5	Entertainment	PI	SPI
7	Auction	PI	FPI
8	Glamour	PI	SPI
12	Global Level	PI	SPI
16	High Profile	PI	SPI
15	Format	PI	FPI
21	Star owners	PI	SPI
23	Contests	PI	FPI
22	International Players	PI	SPI
25	Music	PI	FPI
10	Fixing	DI	UDI
9	Controversial	DI	UDI
13	Players' Conflict	DI	UDI
6	Cheer Girls	DI	UDI
11	Parties	DI	RDI
14	Not a gentlemen sport	DI	UDI
19	BCCI	DI	RDI
18	Overdose of cricket	DI	RDI
20	Black Money	DI	UDI
17	Betting	DI	UDI
24	Conflict of interest	DI	RDI

Table 11: Females High Versus Experts I

Same Positive Influencers were 10; Ironically, Flip Positive Influencers were 4;

The similar perception on influencers, which were Doppelgänger, was on 7; Whereas Reversal of Doppelgänger Influencers was on 4. This shows an overlap of Positive Influencers to the extent of 71.4% (a moderate high). But the overlap on doppelgänger Influencers is only 63.63%

On an advanced level, the combined ESIL ratings are more revealing as they incorporate criticality in BANV maps.

		Experts	Females High	
Positive Influencers				**Beta**
	Same SPI	668.491	478.335	0.716
	Flip FPI	193.618	86.376	0.446
	Overall	508.323	383.411	0.754
Doppelgangers				
	Unchanged UDI	184.656	173.326	0.939
	Reversed RDI	107.901	146.102	1.354
	Overall	187.915	141.708	0.754
Overall		201.978	152.359	0.754

Table 12: Females High Versus Experts II

*Beta is the ratio of category ESIL per influencer to the same for Experts. A low beta means very different perception; a high beta implicates commonality of perception.

#Again an Overall low beta implies that segment views the brand as very weak compared to the Experts judgment, esp. as the negativity of Effective doppelgänger (UDI and FPI) is applied.

- Notable here is, the target category tends to underplay the SPIs by 28.4%.
- The FPIs have got a big reversal of 55.4%.
- The UDIs have experienced a reversal, falling by only 6.1%
- The reversed RDIs have gone through a big 35.4% inflation.
- This depicts the gross error a brand custodian may have committed by moving on perception of Experts.

(4) Females Low Versus Experts:

Item Code	Entity	Expert	Females Low
1	Cricket	PI	SPI
2	High Paced	PI	SPI
3	20-20	PI	SPI
4	Franchise	PI	SPI
5	Entertainment	PI	SPI
7	Auction	PI	FPI
8	Glamour	PI	FPI
12	Global Level	PI	FPI
16	High Profile	PI	FPI
15	Format	PI	FPI
21	Star owners	PI	SPI
23	Contests	PI	FPI
22	International Players	PI	SPI
25	Music	PI	SPI
10	Fixing	DI	RDI
9	Controversial	DI	RDI
13	Players' Conflict	DI	RDI
6	Cheer Girls	DI	RDI
11	Parties	DI	RDI
14	Not a gentlemen sport	DI	RDI
19	BCCI	DI	UDI
18	Overdose of cricket	DI	RDI
20	Black Money	DI	UDI
17	Betting	DI	UDI
24	Conflict of interest	DI	RDI

Table 13: Females Low Versus Experts I

Same Positive Influencers were 8; Ironically, Flip Positive Influencers were 6;

The similar perception on influencers, which were Doppelgänger, was on 3 only;

Whereas, Reversal of Doppelgänger Influencers was on 8. This shows an overlap of Positive Influencers to the extent of 57.1% (a mid-value). But the overlap on doppelgänger Influencers is only 27.2%

On an advanced level, the combined ESIL ratings are more revealing as they incorporate criticality in BANV maps.

		Experts	Females Low	
Positive Influencers				Beta
	Same SPI	712.664	621.16	0.872
	Flip FPI	293.012	205.457	0.701
	Overall	447.326	462.682	1.034
Doppelgangers				
	Unchanged U	89.434	92.136	1.03
	Reversed RDI	181.987	304.204	1.672
	Overall	225.153	167.683	0.745
Overall		205.234	235.75	1.149

Table 14: Females Low Versus Experts II

*Beta is the ratio of category ESIL per influencer to the same for Experts. A low beta means very different perception; a high beta implicates commonality of perception.

#Again an Overall low beta implies that segment views the brand as very weak compared to the Experts judgment, esp. as the negativity of Effective doppelgänger (UDI and FPI) is applied.

- Notable here is, the target category tends to underplay the SPIs by 12.8%.
- The FPIs have got a big drubbing of 29.9%.
- The UDIs have experienced a reversal, increasing by a mere 3%
- The reversed RDIs have gone through a massive 67.2% inflation.
- This depicts the gross error a brand custodian may have committed by moving on perception of Experts.

(5) Males Overall Versus Experts:

Item Code	Entity	Expert	Males Overall
1	Cricket	PI	SPI
2	High Paced	PI	SPI
3	20-20	PI	SPI
4	Franchise	PI	SPI
5	Entertainment	PI	SPI
7	Auction	PI	SPI
8	Glamour	PI	SPI
12	Global Level	PI	FPI
16	High Profile	PI	FPI
15	Format	PI	SPI
21	Star owners	PI	SPI
23	Contests	PI	SPI
22	International Players	PI	SPI
25	Music	PI	SPI
10	Fixing	DI	UDI
9	Controversial	DI	RDI
13	Players' Conflict	DI	RDI
6	Cheer Girls	DI	RDI
11	Parties	DI	RDI
14	Not a gentlemen sport	DI	UDI
19	BCCI	DI	UDI
18	Overdose of cricket	DI	UDI
20	Black Money	DI	UDI
17	Betting	DI	UDI
24	Conflict of interest	DI	UDI

Table 15: Males Overall Versus Experts I

Same Positive Influencers were 12; Ironically, Flip Positive Influencers were 2;

The similar perception on influencers, which were Doppelgänger, was on 7; Whereas Reversal of Doppelgänger Influencers was on 4. This shows an overlap of Positive Influencers to the extent of 85.7% (a high). But the overlap on Doppelgänger Influencers is only 63.63%

On an advanced level, the combined ESIL ratings are more revealing as they incorporate criticality in BANV maps.

		Experts	Males Overall	
Positive Influencers				**Beta**
	Same SPI	225.153	447.713	1.988
	Flip FPI	572.849	159.969	0.279
	Overall	292.595	407.629	1.393
Doppelgangers		479.648		
	Unchanged UI	132.004	160.639	1.217
	Reversed RDI	200.043	287.377	1.437
	Overall	167.691	160.49	0.957
Overall		246.606	203.106	0.824

Table 16: Males Overall Versus Experts II

*Beta is the ratio of category ESIL per influencer to the same for Experts. A low beta means very different perception; a high beta implicates commonality of perception.

#Again an Overall low beta implies that segment views the brand as very weak compared to the Experts judgment, esp. as the negativity of Effective doppelgänger (UDI and FPI) is applied.

- Notable here is, the target category tends to exaggerate the SPIs by 98.8%.
- The FPIs have got a big drubbing of 72.1%.
- The UDIs have experienced a reversal, exaggerating by 21.7%
- The reversed RDIs have gone through a massive 43.7% inflation.
- This depicts the gross error a brand custodian may have committed by moving on perception of Experts.

(6) Females Overall Versus Experts

Item Code	Entity	Expert	Females Overall
1	Cricket	PI	SPI
2	High Paced	PI	SPI
3	20-20	PI	SPI
4	Franchise	PI	SPI
5	Entertainm	PI	SPI
7	Auction	PI	FPI
8	Glamour	PI	SPI
12	Global Leve	PI	FPI
16	High Profile	PI	SPI
15	Format	PI	FPI
21	Star owner	PI	SPI
23	Contests	PI	FPI
22	Internation	PI	SPI
25	Music	PI	SPI
10	Fixing	DI	UDI
9	Controvers	DI	RDI
13	Players' Co	DI	UDI
6	Cheer Girls	DI	UDI
11	Parties	DI	RDI
14	Not a gentl	DI	UDI
19	BCCI	DI	UDI
18	Overdose c	DI	RDI
20	Black Mone	DI	UDI
17	Betting	DI	UDI
24	Conflict of i	DI	RDI

Table 17: Females Overall Versus Experts I

Same Positive Influencers were 10; Ironically, Flip Positive Influencers were 4;

The similar perception on influencers, which were Doppelgänger, was on 7; Whereas Reversal of Doppelgänger Influencers was on 4. This shows an overlap of Positive Influencers to the extent of 71.4% (a high). But the overlap on Doppelgänger Influencers is only 63.63%

On an advanced level, the combined ESIL ratings are more revealing as they incorporate criticality in BANV maps.

		Experts	Females Overall	
Positive Influencers				**Beta**
	Same SPI	637.637	509.852	0.8
	Flip FPI	270.753	149.182	0.551
	Overall	490.8	419.373	0.854
Doppelgangers				
	Unchanged U	175.624	215.215	1.225
	Reversed RDI	123.709	193.177	1.562
	Overall	210.216	191.203	0.91
Overall		182.353	150.72	0.827

Table 18: Females Overall Versus Experts II

*Beta is the ratio of category ESIL per influencer to the same for Experts. A low beta means very different perception; a high beta implicates commonality of perception.

#Again an Overall low beta implies that segment views the brand as very weak compared to the Experts judgment, esp. as the negativity of Effective doppelgänger (UDI and FPI) is applied.

- Notable here is, the target category tends to underplay the SPIs by 20%.
- The FPIs have got a big drubbing of 44.9%.
- The UDIs have experienced a reversal, exaggerating by 22.5%
- The reversed RDIs have gone through a massive 56.2% inflation.
- This depicts the gross error a brand custodian may have committed by moving on perception of Experts.

(7) High Overall Versus Exerts:

Item Code	Entity	Expert	High Overall
1	Cricket	PI	SPI
2	High Paced	PI	SPI
3	20-20	PI	SPI
4	Franchise	PI	SPI
5	Entertainm	PI	SPI
7	Auction	PI	SPI
8	Glamour	PI	SPI
12	Global Leve	PI	FPI
16	High Profile	PI	FPI
15	Format	PI	SPI
21	Star owner	PI	SPI
23	Contests	PI	SPI
22	Internation	PI	SPI
25	Music	PI	FPI
10	Fixing	DI	UDI
9	Controvers	DI	RDI
13	Players' Co	DI	RDI
6	Cheer Girls	DI	RDI
11	Parties	DI	RDI
14	Not a gentl	DI	UDI
19	BCCI	DI	UDI
18	Overdose o	DI	RDI
20	Black Mone	DI	UDI
17	Betting	DI	UDI
24	Conflict of i	DI	UDI

Table 19: High Overall Versus Exerts I

Same Positive Influencers were 11; Ironically, Flip Positive Influencers were 3;

The similar perception on influencers, which were Doppelgänger, was on 6; Whereas Reversal of Doppelgänger Influencers was on 5. This shows an overlap of Positive Influencers to the extent of 78.5% (a high). But the overlap on Doppelgänger Influencers is only 54.5%

On an advanced level, the combined ESIL ratings are more revealing as they incorporate criticality in BANV maps.

		Experts	High Overall	
Positive Influencers				**Beta**
	Same SPI	623.793	458.173	0.734
	Flip FPI	199.22	123.354	0.619
	Overall	483.86	395.769	0.818
Doppelgangers				
	Unchanged UI	140.693	130.647	0.929
	Reversed RDI	176.009	258.479	1.469
	Overall	160.202	128.216	0.8
Overall		251.998	207.134	0.822

Table20: High Overall Versus Exerts II

*Beta is the ratio of category ESIL per influencer to the same for Experts. A low beta means very different perception; a high beta implicates commonality of perception.

#Again, an Overall low beta implies that segment views the brand as very weak compared to the Experts judgment, esp. as the negativity of Effective doppelgänger (UDI and FPI) is applied.

- Notable here is, the target category tends to underplay the SPIs by 26.6%.
- The FPIs have got a big drubbing of 38.1%.
- The UDIs have experienced a reversal, falling by 7.1%
- The reversed RDIs have gone through a massive 46.9% inflation.
- This depicts the gross error a brand custodian may have committed by moving on perception of Experts.

(8) Low Overall Versus Experts:

Item Code	Entity	Expert	Low Familiarity Overall
1	Cricket	PI	SPI
2	High Paced	PI	SPI
3	20-20	PI	SPI
4	Franchise	PI	SPI
5	Entertainm	PI	SPI
7	Auction	PI	FPI
8	Glamour	PI	SPI
12	Global Leve	PI	FPI
16	High Profile	PI	FPI
15	Format	PI	SPI
21	Star owner	PI	SPI
23	Contests	PI	FPI
22	Internation	PI	SPI
25	Music	PI	SPI
10	Fixing	DI	RDI
9	Controvers	DI	RDI
13	Players' Co	DI	RDI
6	Cheer Girls	DI	RDI
11	Parties	DI	RDI
14	Not a gentl	DI	RDI
19	BCCI	DI	UDI
18	Overdose o	DI	RDI
20	Black Mone	DI	UDI
17	Betting	DI	UDI
24	Conflict of i	DI	RDI

Table 21: Low Overall Versus Experts I

Same Positive Influencers were 10; Ironically, Flip Positive Influencers were 4;

The similar perception on influencers, which were Doppelgänger, was on 3 alone;

Whereas Reversal of Doppelgänger Influencers was on 8. This shows an overlap of Positive Influencers to the extent of 71.4% (a high). But the overlap on Doppelgänger Influencers is only 27.2%

On an advanced level, the combined ESIL ratings are more revealing as they incorporate criticality in BANV maps.

		Experts	Low Overall	
Positive Influencers				**Beta**
	Same SPI	632.464	528.582	0.836
	Flip FPI	283.685	166.013	0.585
	Overall	432.252	415.478	0.961
Doppelgangers				
	Unchanged U	89.434	88.065	0.985
	Reversed RDI	181.987	274.098	1.506
	Overall	200.435	132.607	0.662
Overall		255.1	262.015	1.027

Table 22: Low Overall Versus Experts II

*Beta is the ratio of category ESIL per influencer to the same for Experts. A low beta means very different perception; a high beta implicates commonality of perception.

#Again an Overall low beta implies that segment views the brand as very weak compared to the Experts judgment, esp. as the negativity of Effective doppelgänger (UDI and FPI) is applied.

- Notable here is, the target category tends to underplay the SPIs by 16.4%.
- The FPIs have got a big drubbing of 41.5%.
- The UDIs have experienced a slight reversal, falling by 1.5%
- The reversed RDIs have gone through a massive 50.6% inflation.
- This depicts the gross error a brand custodian may have committed by moving on perception of Experts.

PAIR-WISE CORRELATIONS

Correlations				
	Males High	Males Low	Females High	Females Low
Males High	1.00	0.84	0.92	0.81
Males Low	0.84	1.00	0.71	0.98
Females High	0.92	0.71	1.00	0.64
Females Low	0.81	0.98	0.64	1.00

	Males Overall	Females Overall	High Familiarity Overall	Low Familiarity Overall
Males Overall	1.00	0.99	0.93	0.95
Females Overall	0.99	1.00	0.92	0.96
High Familiarity Overall	0.93	0.92	1.00	0.78
Low Familiarity Overall	0.95	0.96	0.78	1.00

Table 23: Pair-wise Correlations

These findings are potent for IPL marketing. **It stands uncovered that gender per se bears low correlations.** It's familiarity levels that impact more. The prime IPL marketing so far has been male-centric, presuming males were a central icon in the customer base. This is untrue. Females are as significant. Instead, the familiarity levels have the most potent bearing.

This implies IPL sponsors/ management ought to spend more on educating the masses, and foster a higher level of familiarity with the game. This shall enable a better appreciation of the game, and also help counter sinister Doppelgänger imagery promoted by inimical market forces. Educated customers wouldn't be that easily led astray.

SPLIT-HALF VALIDITY

In order to evaluate validity standard of the tests, every community sample was split into two randomized half of equal size, and its Doppelgänger analysis done. The validation was proven beyond doubt as per the reported correlations.

Split-Half Validity Tables			
	Males High I	Males High II	Males High Overall
Males High I	1	0.98	0.97
Males High II	0.98	1	0.99
Males High Overall	0.97	0.99	1

Table 24: Split-Half Validity

This table indicates a high degree of validation amongst the Males High 2 randomized groups. This also matches correlation overall.

Split-Half Validity Tables			
	Males Low I	**Males Low II**	**Males Low Overall**
Males Low I	1	0.99	0.97
Males Low II	0.99	1	0.95
Males Low Overall	0.97	0.95	1

Table 25: Split-Half Validity Tables I

This table indicates a high degree of validation amongst the Males Low 2 randomised groups. Thus proven that the research had robustness and is valid with a high degree of confidence.

Split-Half Validity Tables			
	Females High I	**Females High II**	**Females High Overall**
Females High I	1	0.99	0.99
Females High II	0.99	1	0.99
Females High Overall	0.99	0.99	1

Table 26: Split-Half Validity Tables II

This table indicates a high degree of validation amongst the Females High 2 randomised groups. The groups correlate highly.

		Split-Half Validity Tables					
		Females Low I		Females Low II		Females Low Overall	
Females Low I		1		0.98		0.98	
Females Low II		0.98		1		0.98	
Females Low Overall		0.98		0.98		1	

Table 27: Split-Half Validity Tables III

This table indicates a high degree of validation amongst the Females Low 2 randomised groups. So the aggregation has a high validity.

		Split-Half Validity Tables			
	Males I		**Males II**		**Males Overall**
Males I	1		0.99		0.99
Males II	0.99		1		0.99
Males Overall	0.99		0.99		1

Table 28: Split-Half Validity Tables IV

This table indicates a high degree of validation amongst the Males 2 randomised groups. There is no partitioning within the category.

Split-Half Validity Tables				
	Females I	Females II	Females Overall	
Females I	1	0.98	0.97	
Females II	0.98	1	0.95	
Females Overall	0.97	0.95	1	

Table 29: Split-Half Validity Tables Split-Half Validity Tables V

This table indicates a high degree of validation amongst the Females 2 randomised groups. The aggregation has thus a strong validity.

	Low I	Low II	Low Overall
Low I	1	0.97	0.96
Low II	0.97	1	0.95
Low Overall	0.96	0.95	1

Table 30: Split-Half Validity Tables VI

This table indicates a high degree of validation amongst the Low Familiarity High 2 randomised groups. This is little low then that of gender based communities, but even then is very high and acceptable.

Split-Half Validity Tables

	High I	High II	High Overall	
High I	1	0.96	0.94	
High II	0.96	1	0.92	
High Overall	0.94	0.92	1	

Table 31: Split-Half Validity Tables (High – High)

This table indicates a high degree of validation amongst the High Familiarity 2 randomised groups. Somewhat lower correlates than amongst genders; nevertheless pretty high.

CONTRIBUTION OF THE RESEARCH

This portion attempts to list how useful this research has been and can be to other researchers. It also points out what's the relevance of this research and fitment within extant body of knowledge.

Today's forward-leaning marketers understand that relevance isn't pegged to temporality. A relevant, well-positioned brand is one that is alive and dynamic, restless and unceasingly moving forward. It continues to challenge itself and reorients itself to all focus target groups. It's the target groups, which are the eventual reason for existence of a brand, its raison d'être. Loyalty is an outcome of first being considerate to needs and perception of target communities.

- This research has brought in a better appreciation of Doppelgänger imagery
- This has paved path for an analytic and empirical measurement of impact of Doppelgänger imagery.
- Thus brands can keep a quantitative tab on influence of Doppelgänger.
- The apparent myth of what constitutes Doppelgänger and what not has been shattered. The correct reading as per general consumer, rather than critic or experts basis labelling has been encouraged.
- The correlations and validity of findings as per varied segment of consumers has been showcased lucidly.
- Firms can thus take proactive initiatives to counter Doppelgänger elements of brand.

EXTENDING TO OTHER BRANDS

The further fructification would result from extending this research and its process/ model to other brands. It shall corroborate and even point out shortcomings, if any, left behind. Achieving brand appropriateness means that companies have to make sure they are obsessed with their customers and indeed value insights about target groups' sensibilities. After all, customer is the true king/ queen. This churn and introspection would excite fresh ideas, be agile enough to implement. This is how customer delight can be truly pursued and attained. This means accepting that in today's fast-paced, hyper-connected, peer influenced world, business models are challenged daily.

It requires speaking with one voice, across all channels and all levels. This research permits this, at a granular level, down to whatever influencers we wish to incorporate in the messaging. This is a beautiful tool in a complex real world, sufficiently analytic tool that this is. The unison in voices/ messaging can be attained, and a seamless campaigning launched.

This shall eliminate fragmented attacks by brad custodians. This would also lower need for heuristics, bringing forth precise calibrated perceptions.

This is probably the most singular contribution of this research. So far, there was no analytic treatment applied to the grasp of Doppelgänger of a brand. This study has delved in that direction, and laid forward a process to analytically grasp the Doppelgänger

It has opened the qualitative concept to quantitative crunching and calibration

It has segregated various customers into meaningful chunks, and establishing their Doppelgänger s, it has yielded tools to tweak them.

It not only reveals the underlying Doppelgänger imagery, it provisions tools to undo or aggravate the same – this is a very useful outcome. Thus we needn't wait passively afore Doppelgänger as a ever harming monster. Instead, we can cut the monster to size, or even enhance its stature.

THE INFLUENCERS INTEGRATED DOPPELGÄNGER BRAND MODEL

The journey behind this research has been a beautiful experience. It has allowed a deep study of elements of brand perception in eyes of various target communities. The empirically born brand measurement process has been proven to be robust, and shall be useful for other brands. It integrates evaluating impact of all influencers, whether positive or negative, as per intensity in the lattice of associated network. It also enables a laser focused tweaking of a specific target community as a preferred community, as the brand custodian may decide time to time. Specific campaigns designated to enhance the brand in eyes of a target community can be envisaged and after the due creativity has been woven in, an analytical evaluation of the campaign(s) can be rolled out.

This model has been evolved as a build-up on the earlier work done by greats like BANV models. But never before, was this taken to measure Doppelgänger elements influence. Nor were there a standardized methodology to perform the process.

Now the brand custodians can administer this model and the concomitant process and stand up for objective scrutiny. The subjectivity in campaigns, hitherto a great barrier in linking with business results, can thus be offset with ease.

THE PROCESS:

Step 1. Choose the brand to be evaluated.

Step 2. List its multiple influencers.

Step 3. Formulate a team of experts who have a high level understanding of the brand.

Step 4. The team enumerates multiple influencers, as many as they can brainstorm.

Step 5 Decide respondents as representatives of target groups. The beauty is various target groups can be carved out of the respondents even later on.

Step 6. The chosen subset of the respondents evolves the brand association networks as per their understanding. This is a very democratic input, and is not subverted by anyone in any direction.

Step 7. Analysis of the networks allows curtailing the influencers to a manageable number. The model is robust and allows for any number of influencers. Thus degrees of freedom can be theoretically infinite.

Step 8. All the respondents now submit their brand association networks as per finalized list of priority influencers.

Step 9. The BANV values are computed and aggregated.

Step 10. The comparison of Target community with Experts' labeling of Positive Influencers and Doppelgänger Influencers is done into four zones:

- Same perception on positives SPI
- Flip perception on positives FPI, effectively making these Doppelgänger in eyes of the target community
- Same perception Doppelgänger UDI
- Reversed perception Doppelgänger effectively making them positive influencers RDI

Step 11. Averaging per influencer BANV scores for each of four zones, clubbing the SPI with RDI, and also clubbing the UDI with FPI.

Step 12. Overall BANV as a singular score of the brand per influencer is measured out.

Step 13. This process can be carried out as frequently as desirable and map a campaign's efficacy at various points of time in its life cycle.

Step 14. Specific influencer's status can be monitored by periodic studies and zeroed in upon.

In conclusion, the elaborate but simple to administer process shall permit graphic portrayal of a brand as dependent on its influencers.

This can be utilized both by brand custodians, and also by brand assaulters. Brand custodians can build safeguards against attack by working on flip/ reversal of influencers, while trying to preserve the positive ones. Conjoint formulations for mix of categories can also be performed with ease. Even focusing on a single of few clients in B2B could be done as the methodology is independent of size of respondents.

RECOMMENDATIONS

We all know it's exceptionally difficult to build a great brand. And on top of that, build a brand that consistently inspires, influences and compels. The existential purpose of a brand is that it gets customers to not only buy more and spend more but to advocate more. This naturally requires a target group focus, with conjoint target groups chosen for priority messaging.

Strategy implies one cannot and shouldn't say yes to everything. One has to willy-nilly say yes to a target group, and therein also say a moderate no to other target group. Trying to be a universally accepted brand is contrary to brand's structural characteristic via positioning, and differentiation.

Successful brands push themselves to continuously be what we the target groups wish them to be. This research has allowed evolution of a robust methodology, model, and process towards the same.

Having affirmed this, we have come to know that, for IPL as a focus brand:

- Critics or experts labeling of brand elements cannot be taken on face value
- The viewpoint of various consumer segments is more important as they are the ones which drive a brand's business
- The viewpoint of consumer segments can vary from that of experts
- There may be high or low correlations in perceptions of segments
- Doppelgänger should be empirically measured as illustrated in this study
- This yields a methodology to analytically sculpt a brand's perception in the market, despite it having a few Doppelgänger elements.
- Males High Familiarity segment had the highest correlation with Females High Familiarity, and the least with Females Low Familiarity one
- Males Low Familiarity segment had the highest correlation in perception as measured by BANV values with Females Low Familiarity one.
- The genders didn't have as high a correlation as the degree of familiarity operated as a remarkable feature
- Aggregation of genders across familiarity seemed to neutralize any differences
- But aggregation of familiarity served as a differentiator with distinct perceptions.
- The consonance grids are a appropriate tool to manage strategy element by element as per target segments.

https://www.forbes.com/sites/scottdavis/2015/01/12/3-steps-to-building-relentless-brand-relevance/#740b99477cf4

SCOPE FOR FUTURE RESEARCH

Business revolutions once had a bit of continuity to them. The Industrial Revolution lasted for decades, the postindustrial revolution had a solid 20-year run, and even the dot-com revolution persevered for a good five years. But no more so. It's disruptive now, innovation breaks new barriers by the minute.

Demands are in state of flux, and ever evolving. To meet these exacting desires, new and different products and services appear unceasingly. Brand new categories and subcategories come into existence almost overnight, as existing ones change or fade. Newer categories also emerge in target communities. There is a change naturally in

attribute of the company's products, services, and brands.

As times change, the relevance is fundamentally unlike the characteristics traditionally associated with a brand's potency. A brand seems strong because tracking studies show that it retains a high level of trust, esteem, perceived quality, and maybe even perceived innovativeness. Customers remain satisfied and loyal. However, its market share may be slipping — perhaps significantly — and fewer customers, particularly new customers, are considering it.

In today's environment, a brand needs to be better-understood at the most granular levels. A broad based grasp of a brand isn't adequate as communities fragmentize, social structures break in society. This all point to the drift further research ought to take.

- Application of the methodology portrayed herein can be done by other researchers and thus standardised further.
- The framework shared herein shall become more robust with findings of similar research into other mega and small brands.
- Doppelgänger imagery as tinkered with handling initiatives can be modelled and scenarios analytically mapped without actually bearing brunt of experimentation.
- Different researches can be rolled out in product and service oriented brands.
- Correlating multiple target communities can yield practical insights in brand management.
- Similar research in different geographies shall proffer culturally tuned reserve of data that can be instrumental in launch of new brands.

- Employing this framework, defenses can be built against anticipated doppelgänger attacks
- The product life cycle doppelgänger as per different stages of the brand ought to be studied for better control on brand in hands of a brand custodian.

❐

REFERENCES

Aaker, D. A. (2012). *Building strong brands*. Simon and Schuster.

Aaker, D. A. (1992). Managing brand equity: capitalizing on the value of a brand name. *Journal of Marketing, 56*(2), 125-128.

Aaker, D. A. (2010). *Brand relevance: Making competitors irrelevant*. John Wiley & Sons.

Aaker, D. A., & Jacobson, R. (1994). The financial information content of perceived quality. *Journal of marketing research*, 191-201.

Aaker, J., Fournier, S., & Brasel, S. A. (2004). When good brands do bad. *Journal of Consumer research, 31*(1), 1-16.

Abi-Ezzi, N. (2000). *An analysis of the treatment of the double in the work of Robert Louis Stevenson, Wilkie Collins, and Daphne du Maurier* (Doctoral dissertation, University of London).

Aggarwal, P., & McGill, A. L. (2007). Is that car smiling at me? Schema congruity as a basis for evaluating anthropomorphized products. *Journal of Consumer Research, 34*(4), 468-479.

Amit Gupta (2011) The IPL and the Indian domination of global cricket, Sport in Society: Cultures, Commerce, Media, Politics, 14:10, 1316-1325

Ajzen, I., & Fishbein, M. (1980). Understanding attitudes and predicting social behaviour.

Arora, R., & Stoner, C. (2009). A mixed method approach to understanding brand personality. *Journal of Product & Brand Management, 18*(4), 272-283.

Batey, M. (2015). *Brand Meaning: Meaning, Myth and Mystique in Today's Brands*. Routledge.

Barreda, A. A., Bilgihan, A., Nusair, K., & Okumus, F. (2015). Generating brand awareness in online social networks. *Computers in Human Behavior, 50*, 600-609.

B Barhorst, J., & Wilson, A. (2017). Retweeting brand experiences: factors motivating receivers to proliferate brand image disruptions.

Belén del Río, A., Vazquez, R., & Iglesias, V. (2001). The effects of brand associations on consumer response. *Journal of consumer marketing, 18*(5), 410-425.

Berger, J. (2016). *Contagious: Why things catch on*. Simon and Schuster.

Berger, J., & Milkman, K. L. (2013). Emotion and virality: what makes online content go viral?. *GfK Marketing Intelligence Review, 5*(1), 18-23.

Berry, L. L. (2000). Cultivating service brand equity. *Journal of the Academy of marketing Science, 28*(1), 128-137.

Bhattacharya, S. O. N. A. L. I., & Bhattacharya, S. H. U. B. H. A. S. H. E. E. S. H. (2012). Auction of players in Indian Premier League: the strategic perspective. *International Journal of Multidisciplinary Research, 2*(2), 16-36.

Biel, A. L. (1993). Converting image into equity. *Brand equity and advertising: Advertising's role in building strong brands*, 67-82.

Brandt, C., Pahud de Mortanges, C., Bluemelhuber, C., & Van Riel, A. (2010). Brand Concept Maps: A Method of Capturing Doppelgänger Brand Image.

Brown, S. (2010). Where the wild brands are: Some thoughts on anthropomorphic marketing. *The Marketing Review, 10*(3), 209-224.

Cammaerts, B. (2007). Jamming the political: beyond counter-hegemonic practices. *Continuum, 21*(1), 71-90.

Carducci, V. (2006). Culture jamming: A sociological perspective. *Journal of Consumer Culture, 6*(1), 116-138.

Chieng, Y. L., & Goi, C. L. (2011). Customer-based brand equity: A study on interrelationship among the brand equity dimension in Malaysia. *African Journal of Business Management, 5*(30), 11856.

Claudy, M. C., Garcia, R., & O'Driscoll, A. (2015). Consumer resistance to innovation—a behavioral reasoning perspective. *Journal of the Academy of Marketing Science, 43*(4), 528-544.

Cobb-Walgren, C. J., Ruble, C. A., & Donthu, N. (1995). Brand equity, brand preference, and purchase intent. *Journal of advertising, 24*(3), 25-40.

Coulter, R. H., & Zaltman, G. (1995). Seeing the voice of the customer: Metaphor-based advertising research. *Journal of advertising research, 35*(4), 35.

David, A. (1996). Building strong brands. *New York: The Free.*

De Chernatony, L., & Dall'Olmo Riley, F. (1998). Defining a" brand": Beyond the literature with experts' interpretations. *Journal of Marketing Management,14*(5), 417-443.

Delgado-Ballester, E., & Luis Munuera-Alemán, J. (2005). Does brand trust matter to brand equity?. *Journal of product & brand management, 14*(3), 187-196.

DeLaure, M., Fink, M., & Dery, M. (Eds.). (2017). *Culture jamming: Activism and the art of cultural resistance*. NYU Press.

Dery, M. (1993). *Culture jamming: Hacking, slashing, and sniping in the empire of signs* (Vol. 25). Westfield, NJ: Open Media.

de Sousa, R. L. (2012, September). Hitchcock's queer doubles. In *Film-Philosophy Conference 2012.*

Dobni, D., & Zinkhan, G. M. (1990). In search of brand image: A foundation analysis. *NA-Advances in Consumer Research Volume 17.*

Earle, Carey (2002), "FWD: This Made Me Laugh: How Viral Brand Parodies Impact Your Brand," (accessed September 1, 2005), [available at http://www.brandchannel.com/images/ papers/FWD.pdf].

Edelman, D. C. (2010). Branding in the digital age. *Harvard business review, 88*(12), 62-69.

Enderwick, P., & Nagar, S. (2010). The Indian Premier League and Indian Cricket: Innovation in the face of tradition. *Journal of Sponsorship, 3*(2).

Fayrene, C. Y., & Lee, G. C. (2011). Customer-based brand equity: A literature review. *Researchers World, 2*(1), 33.

Fishbein, M., & Ajzen, I. (1981). On construct validity: A critique of Miniard and Cohen's paper. *Journal of Experimental Social Psychology, 17*(3), 340-350.

Fonseca, T. (2006). The Doppelgänger . *Icons of horror and the supernatural: an encyclopedia of our worst nightmares, 1*, 187-214.

Fournier, S., & Avery, J. (2011). The uninvited brand. *Business horizons, 54*(3), 193-207.

Freud, S. (2004). The uncanny. *Fantastic Literature: A Critical Reader*, 74-101.

Freund, J., & Jacobi, E. S. (2013). Revenge of the brand monsters: How Goldman Sachs' doppelgänger turned monstrous. *Journal of Marketing Management, 29*(1-2), 175-194.

Füller, J., Lüdicke, M. K., & Jawecki, G. (2008). How brands enchant: Insights from observing community driven brand creation. *Advances in consumer research, 35*, 359-366.

Gabl, S., Wieser, V. E., & Hemetsberger, A. (2016). "Will We Hate Google One Day?" a Convention Theory Perspective on Public Brand Evaluations. *ACR North American Advances.*

Giesler, M. (2012). How doppelgänger brand images influence the market creation process: Longitudinal insights from the rise of botox cosmetic. *Journal of Marketing, 76*(6), 55-68.

Gilson, E. (2012). Doppelgänger in Post-Wende Literature: Klaus Schlesinger's Trug and Beyond. *PINFOLD, DEBBIE/SAUNDERS, ANNA (HG.): After the Wall. Remembering and Rethinking the GDR. Basingstoke: Palgrave Macmillan*, 83-97.

Gladwell, M. (2006). *The tipping point: How little things can make a big difference.* Little, Brown.

Gobe, M. (2001). Emotional branding. *The New Paradigm of Connecting Brands to People. New York.*

Grace, D., & O'Cass, A. (2002). Brand associations: looking through the eye of the beholder. *Qualitative Market Research: An International Journal, 5*(2), 96-111.

Grime, I., Diamantopoulos, A., & Smith, G. (2002). Consumer evaluations of extensions and their effects on the core brand: Key issues and research propositions. *European journal of marketing, 36*(11/12), 1415-1438.

Guillory, J. (2010). Genesis of the media concept. *Critical Inquiry, 36*(2), 321-362.

Gupta, A. (2017). Cricket: The Indianization of an Imperial Game. *The Oxford Handbook of Sports History*, 213.

Gupta, A., Naik, A. Y., & Arora, N. (2013). Mapping Sponsorship-linked Marketing in Indian Premier League. *IIM Kozhikode Society & Management Review*, *2*(1), 61-72.

Guthrie, S. E. (1995). *Faces in the clouds: A new theory of religion*. Oxford University Press.

Harold, C. (2004). Pranking rhetoric: "Culture jamming" as media activism. *Critical Studies in Media Communication*, *21*(3), 189-211.

Hearn, K., Mahncke, R. J., & Williams, P. A. (2009, December). Culture jamming: From activism to hactivism. In *Australian Information Warfare and Security Conference* (p. ٣).

Hoeffler, S., & Keller, K. L. (2003). The marketing advantages of strong brands. *The Journal of Brand Management*, *10*(6), 421-445.

Hogg, M. K. (1998). Anti-constellations: exploring the impact of negation on consumption. *Journal of Marketing Management*, *14*(1-3), 133-158.

Hollenbeck, C. R., & Zinkhan, G. M. (2010). Anti-brand communities, negotiation of brand meaning, and the learning process: The case of Wal-Mart. *Consumption, Markets and Culture*, *13*(3), 325-345.

Holt, D. B.. (2002). Why Do Brands Cause Trouble? A Dialectical Theory of Consumer Culture and Branding. *Journal of Consumer Research*, *29*(1), 70–90.

Holt, D., & Cameron, D. (2010). *Cultural strategy: Using innovative ideologies to build breakthrough brands*. Oxford University Press.

Hsieh, M. H. (2002). Identifying brand image dimensionality and measuring the degree of brand globalization: A cross-national study. *Journal of International Marketing*, *10*(2), 46-67.

Iles III, D. M. (2013). *The Contentious Performances of Culture Jamming: Art, Repertoires of Contention, and Social Movement Theory* (Doctoral dissertation, Louisiana State University).

Jalilvand, M. R., Samiei, N., & Mahdavinia, S. H. (2011). The effect of brand equity components on purchase intention: An application of Aaker's model in the automobile industry. *International business and management*, *2*(2), 149-158.

Jean, S. (2011). Brand parody: a communication strategy to attack a competitor. *Journal of Consumer Marketing*, *28*(1), 19-26.

John, D. R., Loken, B., Kim, K., & Monga, A. B. (2006). Brand concept maps: A methodology for identifying brand association networks. *Journal of marketing research*, *43*(4), 549-563.

Johnson, A. R., Matear, M., & Thomson, M. (2011). A coal in the heart: Self-relevance as a post-exit predictor of consumer anti-brand actions. *Journal of Consumer Research*, *38*(1), 108-125.

Kadapa, S. S. (2013). How Sustainable is the Strategy of the Indian Premier League-IPL? A Critical Review of 10 Key Issues that Impact the IPL Strategy.

Kapferer, J. N. (2012). *The new strategic brand management: Advanced insights and strategic thinking*. Kogan page publishers.

Kardes, F. R., Cronley, M. L., & Cline, T. W. (2011). *Consumer Behavior, Mason, OH: South-Western, Cengage Learning, 2011*. ISBN 978-0-538-74540-6.

Kay, M. J. (2006). Strong brands and corporate brands. *European Journal of Marketing*, *40*(7/8), 742-760.

Keller, K. L. (1993). Conceptualizing, measuring, and managing customer-based brand equity. *the Journal of Marketing*, 1-22.

Keller, K. L. (1998). Branding perspectives on social marketing. *NA-Advances in Consumer Research Volume 25.*

Keller, K. L. (2001). *Building customer-based brand equity: A blueprint for creating strong brands* (pp. 72-68). Cambridge, MA: Marketing Science Institute.

Keller, K. L. (2003). Brand synBook: The multidimensionality of brand knowledge. *Journal of consumer research*, *29*(4), 595-600.

Keller, K. L. (2003). Understanding brands, branding and brand equity. *Interactive Marketing*, *5*(1), 7-20.

Klein, N., & Byam, B. (2000). *No logo: Taking aim at the brand bullies* (pp. 1330-1328). Canadian National Institute for the Blind.

Klein, N. (2000). Culture jamming: Ads under attack. *Brandweek*, *41*(28), 28-35.

Kozinets, R. V., & Handelman, J. M. (2004). Adversaries of consumption: Consumer movements, activism, and ideology. *Journal of consumer research*, *31*(3), 691-704.

Krishnamurthy, S., & Kucuk, S. U. (2009). Anti-branding on the internet. *Journal of Business Research*, *62*(11), 1119-1126.

Kuhn, K. A. L., Alpert, F., & Pope, N. K. L. (2008). An application of Keller's brand equity model in a B2B context. *Qualitative Market Research: An International Journal*, *11*(1), 40-58.

Kucuk, S. U. (2008). Negative double jeopardy: The role of anti-brand sites on the internet. *Journal of Brand Management*, *15*(3), 209-222.

Kucuk, S. U. (2016). What Is Brand Hate?. In *Brand Hate* (pp. 36-17). Springer International Publishing.

Kucuk, S. U. (2016). Consequences of Brand Hate. In *Brand Hate* (pp. 66-57). Springer International Publishing.

Kucuk, S. U. (2016). Managing Brand Hate. In *Brand Hate* (pp. -125 136). Springer International Publishing.

Kucuk, S. U. (2016). What Is Hate?. In *Brand Hate* (pp. 15-1). Springer International Publishing.

Lassar, W., Mittal, B., & Sharma, A. (1995). Measuring customer-based brand equity. *Journal of consumer marketing, 12*(4), 11-19.

Lakshman, C., & Akhter, M. (2013). Corporate governance scandals in the Indian Premier League (IPL): Implications for labour. *Labour & Industry: a journal of the social and economic relations of work, 23*(1), 89-106.

Lee, M. S., Motion, J., & Conroy, D. (2009). Anti-consumption and brand avoidance. *Journal of Business Research, 62*(2), 169-180.

Lee, Z., McCloskey, J., & Beverland, M. (2015). "It'S a Bit of a Mask, It'S Not Pure… It'S Not What I Thought": How Doppelgänger Brand Images Attack Brand Authenticity. *ACR Asia-Pacific Advances.*

Low, G. S., & Lamb Jr, C. W. (2000). The measurement and dimensionality of brand associations. *Journal of Product & Brand Management, 9*(6), 350-370.

Luedicke, M. K., & Giesler, M. (2008). Contested consumption in everyday life. *ACR North American Advances.*

Luedicke, M. K., Thompson, C. J., & Giesler, M. (2009). Consumer identity work as moral protagonism: How myth and ideology animate a brand-mediated moral conflict. *Journal of Consumer Research, 36*(6), 1016-1032.

McCaughey, M., & Ayers, M. D. (Eds.). (2013). *Cyberactivism: Online activism in theory and practice.* Routledge.

Mehrabian, A. (1971). *Silent messages* (Vol. 8). Belmont, CA: Wadsworth.

Menon, V. P., & Barani, G. (2016). Dimensions of Brand Equity: An Investigation on Higher Education Institutions. *Asian Journal of Research in Social Sciences and Humanities, 6*(5), 353-359.

Micali, S. (2010). The Hero and His Shadow. *Image & Narrative, 11*(3), 99-110.

Milstein, T., & Pulos, A. (2015). Culture jam pedagogy and practice: Relocating culture by staying on one's toes. *Communication, Culture & Critique, 8*(3), 395-413.

Østergaard, P., Hermansen, J., & Fitchett, J. (2015). Structures of brand and anti-brand meaning: A semiotic square analysis of reflexive consumption. *The Journal of Brand Management, 22*(1), 60-77.

Parker, D., Burns, P., & Natarajan, H. (2008). Player valuations in the Indian premier league. *Frontier Economics, 116.*

Parmentier, M. A., & Fischer, E. (2014). Things fall apart: The dynamics of brand audience dissipation. *Journal of Consumer Research, 41*(5), 1228-1251.

Peretti, J., & Micheletti, M. (2011). The Nike sweatshop email: Political consumerism, internet, and culture jamming. *Politics, Products, and Markets. Exploring Political Consumerism Past and Present. New Brunswick,* 127-142.

Pfeffer, J., Zorbach, T., & Carley, K. M. (2014). Understanding online firestorms: Negative word-of-mouth dynamics in social media networks. *Journal of Marketing Communications, 20*(1-2), 117-128.

Radford, B. (2016). *Bad Clowns.* UNM Press.

Reder, L. M., & Anderson, J. R. (1980). A partial resolution of the paradox of interference: The role of integrating knowledge. *Cognitive Psychology, 12*(4), 447-472.

Ries, A. and Trout,J. (1981) *Positioning, The battle for your mind,* Warner Books – McGraw-Hill Inc., New York, 1981

Romani, S., Grappi, S., Zarantonello, L., & Bagozzi, R. P. (2015). The revenge of the consumer! How brand moral violations lead to consumer anti-brand activism. *The Journal of Brand Management, 22*(8), 658-672.

Roth, M. S. (1995). The effects of culture and socioeconomics on the performance of global brand image strategies. *Journal of Marketing Research,* 163-175.

Rowley, J., & Edmundson-Bird, D. (2013). Brand presence in digital space. *Journal of Electronic Commerce in Organizations (JECO), 11*(1), 63-78.

Sandlin, J. A. (2007). Popular culture, cultural resistance, and anticonsumption activism: An exploration of culture jamming as critical adult education. *New Directions for Adult and Continuing Education, 2007*(115), 73-82.

Saikia, H., Bhattacharjee, D., & Bhattacharjee, A. (2012). Is IPL responsible for cricketers' performance in Twenty20 World Cup. *International Journal of Sports Science and Engineering, 6*(2), 96-110.

Schneider, S. (1999). Monsters as (uncanny) metaphors: Freud, Lakoff, and the representation of monstrosity in cinematic horror. *Other Voices, 1*(3), 1999.

Schnittka, O., Sattler, H., & Zenker, S. (2012). Advanced brand concept maps: A new approach for evaluating the favorability of brand association networks. *International Journal of Research in Marketing, 29*(3), 265-274.

Shin, J. (2008, March). Morality and Internet Behavior: A study of the Internet Troll and its relation with morality on the Internet. In *Society for information technology & teacher education international conference* (pp. 2840-2834). Association for the Advancement of Computing in Education (AACE).

Sivitanides, M., & Shah, V. (2011). The era of digital activism. In *Conference for Information Systems Applied Research* (Vol. 4, pp. 8-1).

Sood Gaurav & Sharma J K, American International Journal of Research in Humanities, Arts and Social Sciences, 12(2), September-November, 2015 pp. 241-245.

Sood G. *et al.*, American International Journal of Research in Humanities, Arts and Social Sciences, 16(3), September-November, 2016, pp. 201-206

Sengupta, S. (1990). Brand positioning. *New Pelhi: Tata McGraw-Hill Publishing Company.*

Stevenson, R. L. (1927). *The Strange Case of Dr. Jekyll and Mr. Hyde* (Vol. 1). Library of Alexandria.

Suler, J. (2004). The online disinhibition effect. *Cyberpsychology & behavior*, *7*(3), 321-326.

Thompson, C. J., Rindfleisch, A., & Arsel, Z. (2006). Emotional branding and the strategic value of the doppelgänger brand image. *Journal of Marketing*,*70*(1), 50-64.

Travis, D. (2001). Branding in the digital age. *Journal of Business Strategy*, *22*(3), 14-18.

Trout, J., (1969) ""Positioning" is a game people play in today's me-too market place", *Industrial Marketing*, Vol.54, No.6, (June 1969), pp.51-55

Van den Bergh, J., & Behrer, M. (2016). *How Cool Brands Stay Hot: Branding to Generations Y and Z.* Kogan Page Publishers.

Vardoulakis, D. (2006). The return of negation: the Doppelgänger in Freud's" The'Uncanny'". *SubStance*, *35*(2), 100-116.

Watkins, B. (2014). An Integrated Approach to Sports Branding: Examining the Influence of Social Media on Brand Outcomes. *International Journal of Integrated Marketing Communications*, *6*(2).

Webber, A. J. (1996). *The Doppelgänger: double visions in German literature*. Clarendon Press.

Wood, L. (2000). Brands and brand equity: definition and management. *Management decision*, *38*(9), 662-669.

Yoo, B., Donthu, N., & Lee, S. (2000). An examination of selected marketing mix elements and brand equity. *Journal of the academy of marketing science*, *28*(2), 195-211.

Zaltman, G. (1997). Rethinking market research: Putting people back in. *Journal of marketing Research*, 424-437.

Živković, M. (2000). The Double as the" Unseen" of Culture: Toward a Definition of Doppelgänger. *Facta Universitatis-Linguistics and Literature*, *2*(7), 121-128.

❒

BIBLOGRAPHY

Aaker, D. A. Alexander Biel, eds.(1992), Building Strong Brands.

Aaker, D. A. (1996). Measuring brand equity across products and markets. *California management review, 38*(3), 102-120.

Aaker, J. (1999). The malleable self: The role of self-expression in persuasion.

Aaker, J. L. (1997). Dimensions of brand personality. *Journal of marketing research*, 347-356.

Alexander, J., Crompton, T., & Shrubsole, G. (2011). Think of me as evil? Opening the ethical debates in advertising. *Public Interest Research Centre.*

Ambler, T., & Styles, C. (1996). Brand development versus new product development: towards a process model of extension decisions. *Marketing Intelligence & Planning, 14*(7), 10-19.

Arnold, M. J., Reynolds, K. E., Ponder, N., & Lueg, J. E. (2005). Customer delight in a retail context: investigating delightful and terrible shopping experiences. *Journal of Business Research, 58*(8), 1132-1145.

Asma, S. T. (2011). *On monsters: An unnatural history of our worst fears.* Oxford University Press.

Bailenson, J. N., & Segovia, K. Y. (2010). Virtual doppelgangers: Psychological effects of avatars who ignore their owners. In *Online worlds: Convergence of the real and the virtual* (pp. 186-175). Springer London.

Bailenson, J. N., & Segovia, K. Y. (2010). Virtual doppelgangers: Psychological effects of avatars who ignore their owners. In *Online worlds: Convergence of the real and the virtual* (pp. 186-175). Springer London.

Bailenson, J. N. (2012). Doppelgangers-a new form of self?. *Psychologist, 25*(1), 36-38.

Bakan, J. (2005). *The corporation: The pathological pursuit of profit and power*. London:

Baldinger, A. L., & Rubinson, J. (1996). Brand loyalty: the link between attitude and behavior. *Journal of advertising research, 36*(6), 22-35.

Balmer, J. M., & Gray, E. R. (2003). Corporate brands: what are they? What of them?. *European journal of marketing, 37*(7/8), 972-997.

Banister, E. N., & Hogg, M. K. (2004). Negative symbolic consumption and consumers' drive for self-esteem: The case of the fashion industry. *European Journal of Marketing, 38*(7), 850-868.

Barney, J. (1991). Firm resources and sustained competitive advantage. *Journal of management, 17*(1), 99-120.

Baudrillard, J. (1993). *Symbolic exchange and death* (I. H. Grant, Trans.). London: Sage. Becker, E. (1997). *The denial of death.* New York, NY: Free Press.

Bendixen, M., Bukasa, K. A., & Abratt, R. (2004). Brand equity in the business-to-business market. *Industrial Marketing Management, 33*(5), 371-380.

Berry, L. L. (2000). Cultivating service brand equity. *Journal of the Academy of marketing Science, 28*(1), 128-137.

Bode, L. (2005). Digital doppelgängers. *M/C Journal: A Journal of Media and Culture, 8*(3), 1-4.

Bong Na, W., Marshall, R., & Lane Keller, K. (1999). Measuring brand power: validating a model for optimizing brand equity. *Journal of product & brand management, 8*(3), 170-184.

Brown, A. D. (1997). Narcissism, identity, and legitimacy. *The Academy of Management Review, 22*(3), 643–686. Retrieved from http://www.jstor.org/stable/259409 Brown, E. H. (2010). *Web of debt: The shocking truth about our money system and how we can break free* (4th ed.). Baton Rouge, LA: Third Millennium Press. Brown, S. (2010). Where the wild brands are: Some thoughts on anthropomorphic marketing.

Chernaik, J. (2011). Schumann's Doppelgängers: Florestan and Eusebius revisited. *The Musical Times, 152*(1917), 45-55.

Chaudhuri, A. (1995). Brand equity or double jeopardy?. *Journal of product & brand management, 4*(1), 26-32.

Chaudhuri, A., & Holbrook, M. B. (2001). The chain of effects from brand trust and brand affect to brand performance: the role of brand loyalty. *Journal of marketing, 65*(2), 81-93.

Chaudhuri, A., & Holbrook, M. B. (2001). The chain of effects from brand trust and brand affect to brand performance: the role of brand loyalty. *Journal of marketing, 65*(2), 81-93.

Code, D. L. (1995). Listening for Schubert's "Doppelgängers". *Music Theory Online, 1*(4).

Dennett, D. C. (1996). [BOOK REVIEW] Kinds of minds, towards an understanding of consciousness. *New Statesman, 125*, 44-45.

Diederich, N. A. (2010). Gothic Doppelgangers and Discourse: Examining the Doubling Practice of (Re) marriage in Jane Eyre. *Nineteenth Century Gender Studies, 6.*

Dobscha, S. (1998). The lived experience of consumer rebellion against marketing. *ACR North American Advances.*

Erdem, T., & Swait, J. (2004). Brand credibility, brand consideration, and choice. *Journal of consumer research, 31*(1), 191-198.

Farquhar, P. H., Han, J. Y., & Ijiri, Y. (1991). Recognizing and measuring brand assets. *Report/Marketing Science Institute (USA).*

Feldwick, P. (1996). What is brand equity anyway, and how do you measure it? *Journal of the Market Research Society, 38*(2), 85-105.

Freud, S., & Waelder, R. (1964). *Sigmund Freud.* Martin.

Fiske, S. T., & Linville, P. W. (1980). What does the schema concept buy us? *Personality and Social Psychology Bulletin, 6*(4), 543-557.

Freud, S. (2003). *The 'uncanny'* (D. McLintock & H. Haughton, Trans., Vol. XVII (1917–1919): *An infantile neurosis and other works*). London: Penguin. (Original work published 1919)

Giesler, M. (2007). Conflict and compromise: drama in marketplace evolution. *Journal of Consumer Research, 34*(6), 739-753.

Gilmore, D. D. (2003). *Monsters: Evil beings, mythical beasts, and all manner of imaginary terrors.* Philadelphia: University of Pennsylvania Press. Gobe, M. (2001). *Emotional branding: The new paradigm for connecting brands to people.* New York, NY: Allworth Press.

Gremler, D. D., & Brown, S. W. (1999). The loyalty ripple effect: appreciating the full value of customers. *International Journal of Service Industry Management, 10*(3), 271-293.

Hankinson, G., & Cowking, P. (1995). What do you really mean by a brand? *Journal of brand management, 3*(1), 43-50.

Haskell, A. S. (1971). THE" DOPPELGÄNGERS" IN CHAUCER'S" TROILUS". *Neuphilologische Mitteilungen, 72*(4), 723-734.

Heard, G. (1947). *Doppelgangers: An Episode of the Fourth, the Psychological, Revolution, 1997.* Vanguard Press, Incorporated.

Holt, D. B. (2002). Why do brands cause trouble? A dialectical theory of consumer culture and branding. *Journal of Consumer Research, 29*(1), 70–90. doi: 10.1086/339922

Holt, D. B. (2006). Jack Daniel's America: Iconic brands as ideological parasites and proselytizers. *Journal of Consumer Culture, 6*(3), 355–377. doi:10.1177/1469540506068683 .

Holt, D. B., & Cameron, D. (2010). *Cultural strategy: Using innovative ideologies to build breakthrough brands.* Oxford: Oxford University Press.

Hoyer, W. D., & Brown, S. P. (1990). Effects of brand awareness on choice for common, repeat-purchase product. Journal of consumer research, 17(2), 141-148.

Kapferer, J. N. (1997). Strategic brand management: creating and sustaining brand equity long term, 2. *Auflage, London*.

Kapturkiewicz, J. The Existence of Doppelgängers and Their Significance in the Contemporary Popular Culture on the Basis of The Shining and The Kill.

Kotler, P., & Keller, K. (2012). L.(2006) Marketing management. *Praha: Grada Publishing*.

Lee, M. S., Conroy, D., & Motion, J. (2009). Brand avoidance: a negative promises perspective. *ACR North American Advances*.

Levitt, T. (1981). Marketing intangible products and product intangibles. *Cornell Hotel and Restaurant Administration Quarterly*, *22*(2), 37-44.

Leuthesser, L., Kohli, C. S., & Harich, K. R. (1995). Brand equity: the halo effect measure. *European Journal of Marketing*, *29*(4), 57-66.

Maio Mackay, M. (2001). Evaluation of brand equity measures: further empirical results. *Journal of product & brand management*, *10*(1), 38-51.

Martin, G. S., & Brown, T. J. (1990). In search of brand equity: the conceptualization and measurement of the brand impression construct. *Marketing theory and applications*, *2*(1), 431-438.

McMahon-Coleman, K. (2013). Myriad Mirrors: Doppelgangers and Doubling in The Vampire Diaries.

Moraldo, S. M. (1996). Wandlungen des Doppelgängers. *Shakespeare-ETA Hoffmann-Pirandello, Frankfurt a. M.*

Motameni, R., & Shahrokhi, M. (1998). Brand equity valuation: a global perspective. *Journal of product & brand management*, *7*(4), 275-290.

Nilsen, D. L. (1998). Doppelgangers and doubles in literature: A study in tragicomic incongruity. *Humor: International Journal of Humor Research*.

Oliver, R. L. (1997). Satisfaction a behavioural perspective on the consumer. Irwin/MacGraw Hill.

Robinson. Bankster Games. (2012). Goldman Sachs is the vampire squid. Retrieved from http://www.bankstergames.com / bankster _ monsters. html Bataille, G. (1991).

Serrano, C. (2009). *Monsters, Vampires and Doppelgängers: Innovation and Transformation of Gothic forms in Latin American Narratives* (Doctoral dissertation, University of California, Irvine).

Sterling, R. (Ed.). (2003). *The Book of Doppelgangers*. Wildside Press LLC.

The accursed share (R. Hurley, Trans., Vol. 1: *Consumption*). New York, NY: Zone Books.

The Marketing Review, *10*(3), 209–224. doi:10.1362/146934710x 523078 Carducci, V. (2006). Culture jamming. *Journal of Consumer Culture*, *6*(1), 116–138. doi:10.1177/1469540506062722

Thompson, C. J. (1996). Caring consumers: Gendered consumption meanings and the juggling lifestyle. *Journal of consumer research*, *22*(4), 388-407.

Vázquez, R., Del Rio, A. B., & Iglesias, V. (2002). Consumer-based brand equity: Development and validation of a measurement instrument. *Journal of Marketing management*, *18*(1-2), 27-48.

Vardoulakis, D. (2004). The critique of loneliness: Towards the political motives of the doppelgänger. *Angelaki: Journal of the Theoretical Humanities*, *9*(2), 81–101.

Washburn, J. H., & Plank, R. E. (2002). Measuring brand equity: An evaluation of a consumer-based brand equity scale. *Journal of Marketing Theory and Practice*, *10*(1), 46-62.

Weber, S. (1973). The sideshow, or: Remarks on a canny moment. *MLN*, *88*(6), 1102-1133.

Webster, M. (2006). Merriam-Webster online dictionary.

❐

BCM Respondent 1

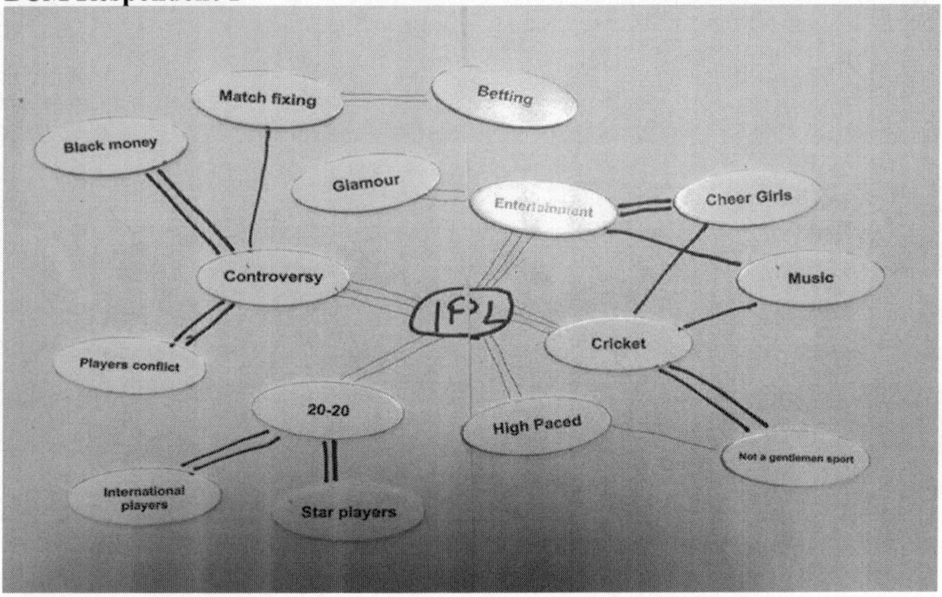

BCM Respondent 2

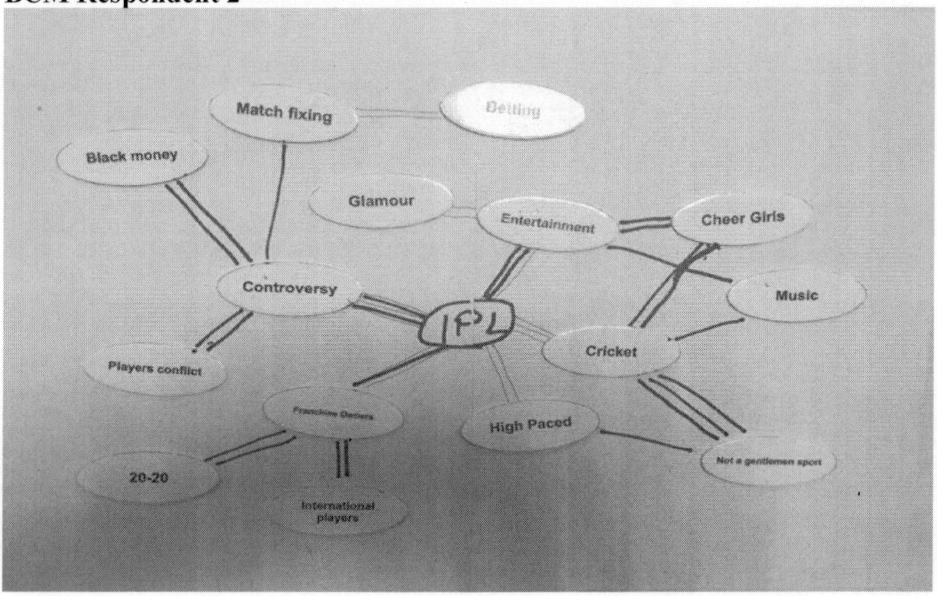

BCM Respondent 3

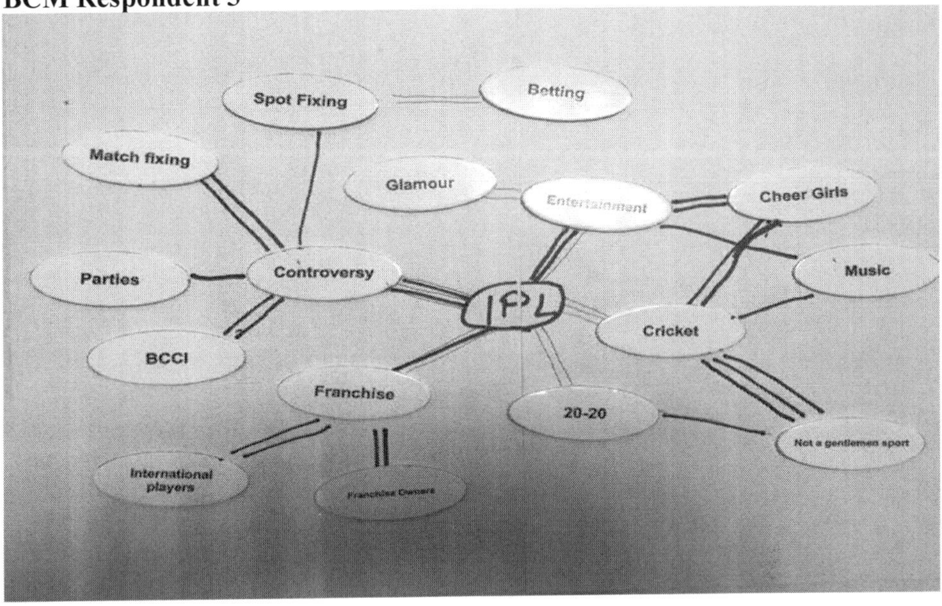

BCM Respondent 41

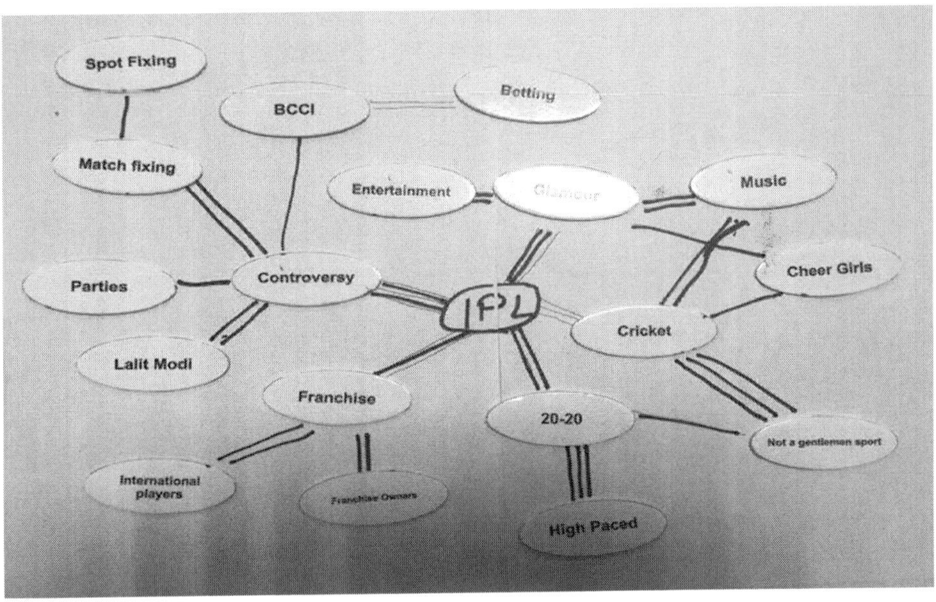

SUBVERSION OF BRAND IMAGE BY ITS MONSTROUS DOPPELGÄNGER

Gaurav Sood
Faculty of Management Studies, Manav Rachna Institute of Research & Studies
J.K. Sharma
Amity Business School, Amity University
and
Sanjay Srivastava
Manav Rachna Institute of Research & Studies

ABSTRACT

This research paper dwell upon the cultural strategy theory, brand psychoanalysis, and literary genealogy in a post-disciplinary manner to analyze the impact of monstrous Doppelgänger brand image by critics of Indian Premiere League (IPL) or Iconic brands. What if unforeseen circumstances hit your established brand? After having invested huge sums of money and many a years in building a brand, what if a tsunami hits your brand akin to Titanic running into hidden icebergs. This paper devolves on the impact of monstrous Doppelgängers on brand, and the consequent subversion of the brand.

The case study of various iconic brands explores how stakeholders/ competition/ critics have been successful or unsuccessful in damaging the image of the leader brands into a 'Monstrous Brand' for a certain stakeholders including large section of consumers. The Doppelgänger brand image, focus negative perceptions against big companies, organizations, people by exploiting their wrong doings and exposing their selfish motives, designs, and effects.

Understanding customers' interpretations of brand image are of paramount concern for both researchers and practitioners of management, business and advertising, as firms strive to boost brand equity and gain/

maintain competitive advantages. Brand equity and brand value are widely discussed in extant studies (for example, Aaker, 1992; Keller, 2003). Doppelgänger Brand Image, an emerging concept in this body of literature holds tremendous potential for deeper forays. Doppelgänger Brand Image, comprising negative perceptions, creates a compelling set of motifs that influence the impact of a brand (Giesler 2012).

As the literature thought dipped into generic and universality of brand and brand image, alongside arose concepts of negative brand Imagery, esp. as a Doppelgänger brand image. The Doppelgänger as a motif arose within German Romanticism and became a canonical theme in the "Gothic" literature. The term was coined by Jean Paul in his novel Siebenkiis, published in 1796 (cited in: Vardoulaki 2004). According to Thompson et al (2006), "Doppelgänger Brand Image is a family of disparaging images and stories about a brand that are circulated in popular culture by a loosely organized network of consumers, anti-brand activists, bloggers, and opinion leaders in the news and entertainment media."

The paper contributes to the theory of Brand Doppelgänger image by showing the importance of cultural jamming as creator of brand doppelganger. The theoretical and managerial implications of monstrous brand doppelgänger and its effect on the contested iconic brands are discussed.

Keywords: doppelgänger brand image; brand psychoanalysis; brand monster; anthropomorphism; Cultural Jamming; Cultural Branding; Brand Image.

DISCOVERING THE MONSTROUS BRAND DOPPELGANGER

Understanding customers' interpretation of brand image is of paramount concern for both researchers and practitioners of management, business and advertising, as firms strive to boost brand equity and gain/ maintain competitive advantages. Brand equity and brand value are widely discussed in extant studies (for example, Aaker, 1996; Keller, 2003; Lassaret et. al., 1995). Professor Jean-Noël Kapferer in 1986 was the first person to come out with the concept of "Brand Identity". He developed a brand identity six sided prism model, which explained the six aspects of brand identity into two dimensions. The first dimension talked about brand as a person and can be explained as brand physique and brand personality and also depicts user reflection and self-image. Second dimension explained a brand's social aspects; its physique, relationship and reflection integrated into the brand personality. According to Kapferer, "Strong brands are capable of weaving all aspects into an effective whole in order to create a concise, clear and appealing brand identity." (Kapferer, 2012). Brand has been the cynosure of most academicians and marketing professionals

– a concept revered and even defined multifariously. Nevertheless, its centrality cannot be overemphasized if one has to conceive or initiate marketing initiatives. Brand is by definition a network of associations in consumers minds (Keller, 2003). Higher the brand equity higher is the consumer preferences and intentions to buy (Cobb-Walgren et al. 1995) and also high brand equity leads to higher stock returns (Aaker and Jacobson, 1994). While Keller (2003) gave the pathway to build brand equity; a conceptual framework to map customer based brand equity was given by Fayrene and Lee (2011). Kuhn (2008) attempted to apply Keller's (2003) B2B branding for commercial and industrial contexts.

Further, imagery based on anthropomorphisation (seeing the human in nonhuman forms and events, suffuses human appraisals (Guthrie 1995)) of products has been a powerful concept; Aggarwal and McGill (2007) have offered a framework to understand the phenomenon of anthropomorphisation of products. They concluded that the consumers positively evaluate products that are presented as humans and have physical characteristics like human beings. Anthropomorphisation portrays a brand as an analogue of man, having a structure or morphology akin to a human being. Brown's (2010) pitch for anthropomorphisation seems very convincing as the best recourse to a larger market share. This is due to a more likely adoption of the brand by marketers and advertisers when the image chosen is an animal, which is "closer" to humanity. However, Holt (2010) has shown how anthropomorphism makes the branding indefensible and even irrelevant for the consumers. He has pioneered the Cultural Strategy Book, while diagnosing failure of brands. He has in fact provided ammunition to the marketer who wants to counter a brand's impending demise by coming up with a disruptive ideology and thus tapping a blue ocean of consumers. Brand image constitutes the most vital element of creation of a brand meaning in the customer's mind (Keller, 2003). Grasping totality of brand image holds some strong, unique, and favorable brand associations in customer's mind in the form of network of associations (John, Keller, 1993, Kim, & Monga, Loken, 2006;). The brand associations networks indicate towards the associations that are linked directly (core associations) or indirectly to the brand and also indicate mutual connect between these brand associations. Naturally, network of associations are a good correlate of a brand's value to consumers (Aaker, 2010; John et al., 2006).

As the literature and advertising thought dipped into generic and universality of brand and brand image, alongside arose concepts of negative brand Imagery, esp. as a Doppelgänger brand image. The Doppelgänger as a concept originated from the German Romanticism and became a widely accepted theme in the "Gothic" literature. The doppelganger terminology was given by Jean Paul in his novel Siebenkiis, published in 1796 (cited in: Vardoulaki 2006). According to Thompson et al (2006), "Doppelgänger Brand Image is a family of disparaging images and stories about a brand that are circulated in popular culture by a loosely organized network of consumers, anti-brand activists, bloggers, and opinion leaders in the news and entertainment media."

Though negativity around brand has not been studied much; many online spaces encouraging anti-consumption and anti-branding have been mapped (Krishnamurthy 2009). There is a study that sheds some fundamental light on why people avoid a particular brand Lee (2009). Harold (2004) has talked of pranksters using media activism to provoke brand custodians. Giesler (2012) tried to get insights in Doppelgänger Brand Image via Botox market analysis over an eight-year period. Creation of Doppelgänger Brand Image for strong brands merits worthy fathoming, since the strong brands are likely to be most vulnerable to lose their brand equity. The synBook of this Doppelgänger Brand Image might perplex customers and can lead to "brand avoidance" effects (i.e., consumers intentionally avoid a brand in question) as described in Thompson et al. (2006). Therefore, this creation of Doppelgänger Brand Image might lead to negative brand imagery, consumer judgment and consequently impact consumer brand's cultural resonance. According to Freund and Jacobi (2013): "The emergence of a powerful, popular Doppelgänger may signal that a brand has peaked and must either evolve or decline." Using Goldman Sachs as a case study, Freund and Jacobi (2013) explored that the stakeholder perception of a company brand is influenced by the generation and circulation of the ugly doppelganger brand imagery by anti-brand activists. This lineage of how organizational personae are created is very insightful.

Thompson et al (2006) integrated Holt's (2010) prime concepts with Doppelgänger Brand Image, showing how the traditionally adopted Emotional Banding lay defunct in face of Doppelgänger Brand Image. As a maverick, Vardoulakis (2006) has given a brave contra- rendition, in delinking Doppelganger with demonic, in fact showing it as having a potential of positivity. This positivity facet is intriguing and requires further study.

Studies on brand image are based on consumer perceptions rather than any rigorously tested measures (Lassar et al., 1995). Aaker & Jacobson (1994) has delineated ways to measure brand, indicating how such a complex construct like brand can be practically measured. Ways to measure Doppelgänger Brand Image have been discussed by Brandt et al (2010) by studying negative user-generated content. Schnittka et al (2012) have validated Brand Concept Maps (John et al 2006) as most appropriate measuring mechanisms.

Doppelgänger Brand Image, an emerging concept in this body of literature holds tremendous potential for deeper forays. Doppelgänger Brand Image is a set of negative perceptions that influence the effect of a brand in the minds of the consumers (Giesler 2012). The proposed research aims to study the impact of creation of Doppelgänger Brand Image on brand imagery; this is well nigh a less explored space. This impact would be measured by systematic and diligent application of rigorous Advanced Brand Concept Mapping network associations (Schnittka et al 2012) .The research not only attempts to identify varied sources of creating a Doppelgänger Brand Image, but also identifies empirically deciphered potency of these influencers in creating the same. Sood G & Sharma J K (2017), have discussed the positive and negative influence of Brand Doppelganger Image using Indian Premier League as a case study by applying Brand Concept Mapping approach.

BRAND AS THE MONSTROUS MR. HYDE

A brand like Dr. Jekyll has two personas, the one the company projects as the brand image and the other what the stakeholders construct as the monstrous doppelganger brand image – the Mr. Hyde. As Dr. Jekyll the brand understands the needs of its customers and provide solution to make their lives better. Whereas, Mr. Hyde, the brand monster will do whatever to sabotage the good brand imagery. Monstrous brand doppelganger is self-serving, negative, devilish, bad and destructive. As a monster, the brand doppelganger without conscience will destroy the very purpose of the brand and feels no remorse for its destructive impact. Monstrous brand doppelganger is the ugly side of the brand, which is created through culture jamming the messages and propagating it through social media. According to the Oxford dictionary "Monster" is, "A large, ugly, and frightening imaginary creature - *a monster with the head of a hyena and hindquarters of a wolf, a world of fable, inhabited by other-worldly monsters"*

Further brand that chooses emotional branding strategies are more vulnerable to the monstrous brand doppelganger. Indian marketers use emotional branding strategies to position their brands in the minds of the customer but the competitors, unsatisfied customers and trolls are culture jamming their emotional branding strategies. A recent example from 2014 Lok Sabha elections testifies the creations of such doppelganger imagery of Congress Vice President Mr. Rahul Gandhi by calling him a "Pappu", "Novice/dumb Prince", "Kid" etc. These trolls originated from the marketing blunders made by Mr. Gandhi giving an opportunity to the opposition parties to ridicule him in public. To ridicule an opposition candidate is a routine act in politics (Thompson, Rindfleisch 2006). Online trollers took this to social media like twitter, facebook, instagram etc. and viral the Rahul Gandhi's doppelganger to a new level, resulting in his and his parties downfall in the 2014 elections.

BRANDING STRATEGIES AND DOPPELGANGER IMAGE

Further this historical evolution of the Doppelgänger brand imagery has emerged from the very existence of the positioning of the brand and can be rooted in the very communication, messaging and mental mapping of the brand. A brand is multidimensional and its linkages and dimensions are worth a study to understand this negative imagery phenomenon called brand Doppelgänger leading to the destruction of a brand. Therefore, to gain better understanding of the imagery of a brand, brand equity, anti-brand activities and cultural jamming concepts became the creator of the brand Doppelgänger phenomenon. The research took a deep foray into these concepts and their impact on the brand with a special emphasis on the rise of the anti-brand activities through stakeholder generated content and activism through offline and digital media particularly the likes of facebook, twitter etc. We also researched the risk associated with the mindshare, emotional and cultural strategies and how through cultural jamming consumers/competition can pull down a brand from a higher ground position. We took a deep dive into lots of brand case studies, books, research papers etc. to understand the approach of the marketers in creating a mouse-trap for consumer buying. One of these concepts was "Mind-share strategy" to develop a consumer mouse-trap. Therefore when brands adopt a mind-share strategy their brand communication is targeted to gain the maximum share of consumers mind space with abstract concepts like "Khushion ki home delivery", "Fanta is FUN", "Youngistaan" etc. The mind-share (a bridge between the functional and emotional benefits) approach implies that consumers value these abstracts and hence are more loyal to brands. Brands rely on these abstract positioning as it is easy to develop, understood and measurable but they are also vulnerable to backlash by consumers for creation of Doppelgänger imagery.

While mind-share and mousetrap strategies have been replaced by emotional and cultural brand strategies but still are vulnerable to consumer backlash resulting in brand Doppelgänger. Where emotional brand strategy is more consumer oriented and relates to consumers inspirations, aspirations and delivers the message in the form of story telling picking up cues from consumers situations and life circumstances. Thompson, Rindfleisch, & Arsel, (2006) argues that; "emotional-branding strategies are conducive to the emergence of a doppelgänger brand image, which is defined as a family of disparaging images and meanings about a brand that circulate throughout popular culture."

On the other hand the cultural branding strategies propagate leaving the red ocean of intense competition and finding a blue ocean through cultural expression. Holt (2010) argues "The engine of cultural innovation is historical change in society that is significant enough to destabilize the category's cultural orthodoxy, creating latent demand for new cultural expressions." Therefore a social disruption can make a brand leader loose and other takes off because of understanding this social change and capitalizing with the right cultural expression. There are many examples like PayTM, Maggie, PVR, IPL etc.

CULTURE JAMMING – A CREATOR OF BRAND DOPPELGANGER IMAGE

Different sources have defined Culture Jamming in their own ways. According to many, Culture Jamming is a form of activism against the political or social system, fake news, subverting, defacing logos, billboards, parody are few forms of culture jamming. Though earlier it use to be a citizen led activism but now it has shifted to consumer led activism viral through social media mainly. Culture Jamming mainly projects consumers concerns regarding exploitation; consumption and experience related to the brand in question but also exposes the dark side of the brand monster. Though there are honest culture jams, which wants to bring attention to some of the negative experiences with the brand but there are others where the purpose is to bring down the leader brand from it's position by maligning its image through culture jamming on social media. Cultural Jamming using memes as a tool – a disparaging image, youtube video, text tweet, facebook post, etc., sarcastic in nature, that is viral by social media users. In the past, big brands advertising messaging were attacked by culture jammers for example, Nike's Swoosh logo memes, Happy Meal by McDonald's (Figure 1) and Coca Cola's Polar Bear campaign memes were targeted.

Figure 1- McDonald's Happy Meal Culture Jamming

Culture Jamming purpose is to challenge the corporate domination in consumer's lives and put them on a defensive and remind them of their corporate social responsibilities. In India, brands that have been targeted by Culture Jammers are Fair & Lovely, Fair & Handsome, Maggie, Airtel, Kingfisher Airline, IPL, PM Narendra Modi, Rahul Gandhi to name a few. Recently both Rahul Gandhi and Narendra Modi were in the news for their twitter popularity index. Twitter has been used by both the political opponents to culture Jam each other's campaign and reports say that Rahul Gandhi's - a leader once ridiculed on twitter by the culture jammers creating a monstrous doppelganger image of the young leader has now improving his twitter scorecard (Figure 2).

Figure 2. Rahul Gandhi's Twitter Scorecard vs Modi & Kejriwal

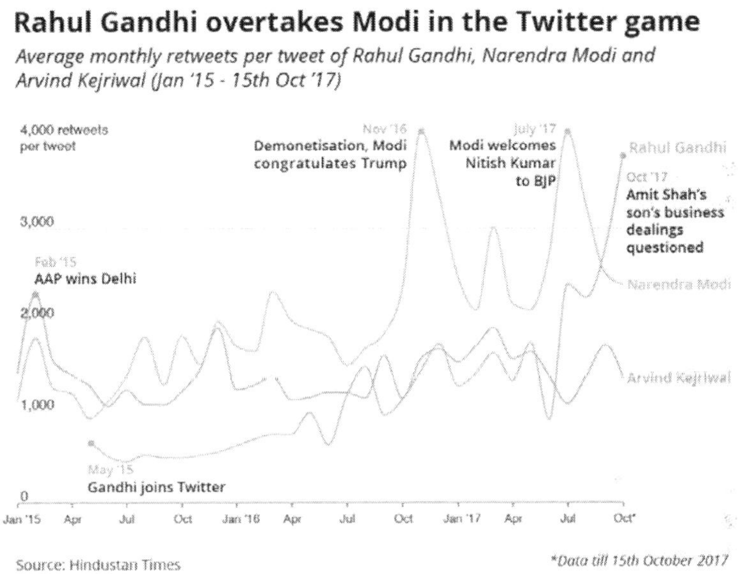

Similarly The Kingfisher Airline Chairman, Dr. Vijay Mallya has been trolled on social media and the hash tag #vijjaymallya have registered 89% negative sentiments (Figure 3).

Figure 3 - #vijaymallya social media sentiment analysis (Oct. 21st, 2017)

Besides leading product and political brands, the monstrous brand doppelganger has also affected negatively India's biggest sporting property – the Indian Premiere League (IPL). Cricket is the king of all the sports in India, cricket carries millions of fan following, viewership and tremendous loyalty. Cricket is popular across masses of all age group and countries. Cricket in India attracts lots of money in the form of sponsorships, ads etc., it is the most richest game in the country. The most famous cricketing event in the world is no doubt the Indian Premier League (IPL), a shorter format 20-20 overs game. Sood G & Sharma J K (2015) have captured the essence of IPL and its' Doppelgänger image, according to them, "Doppelgänger Brand Image is a nouveau construct in the studies of brands and brand values. It maps negative perceptions, which impact a brand, as retaliation to its positive persona. Mapping the evolution of the Doppelgänger imagery, Sood, G & Sharma, J K (2016) laid emphasis on the critical dimensions of the Doppelgänger imagery including brand image, brand equity, anti-branding and culture jamming. These dimensions either influence or get influenced by strong Doppelgänger imagery. Marked with controversies like spot fixing, black money, match fixing, conflict of interests, money game etc., IPL saw a decline in the overall brand value in the year 2012 (Figure 4).

Figure 4 – IPL Brand Value

Year	IPL Brand Value
2010	$ 4.13 billion USD
2011	$ 3.67 billion USD
2012	$ 2.92 billion USD
2013	$ 3.03 billion USD

IPL memes (Figure 5) were circulated by the die-hard fans through there social media accounts and in no time it was viral all over the social network.

Figure 5 - IPL Memes

Source:www.socialsciencecollective.org/ipl,www.news18.com,www.cricketcountry.com

CONCLUSION:

Thus it has been conclusively proven that unless a brand is protected from onslaught by its negative motif, its Doppelgänger, it can be virtually ruined. A negative subversion is surely possible, destroying decades of effort the brand owner might have done over years. The custodians of the brand must try to fend off such attacks, esp. in today's age of social marketing. In this space, no controls work, and even false accusations can be forwarded interminably to unsuspecting consumers, whose opinion can be distorted by what is shared and forwarded. Indeed, this is a serious matter that deserves concentration and organized defensive proactive measures.

REFERENCES

Aaker, D. A. (1992). Managing brand equity: capitalizing on the value of a brand name. *Journal of Marketing*, *56*(2), 125-128.

Aaker, D. A., & Jacobson, R. (1994). The financial information content of perceived quality. *Journal of marketing research*, 191-201.

Aggarwal, P., & McGill, A. L. (2007). Is that car smiling at me? Schema congruity as a basis for evaluating anthropomorphized products. *Journal of Consumer Research*, *34*(4), 468-479.

Brandt, C., Pahud de Mortanges, C., Bluemelhuber, C., & Van Riel, A. (2010). Brand Concept Maps: A Method of Capturing Doppelgänger Brand Image.

Brown, S. (2010). Where the wild brands are: Some thoughts on anthropomorphic marketing. *The Marketing Review*, *10*(3), 209-224.

Cobb-Walgren, C. J., Ruble, C. A., & Donthu, N. (1995). Brand equity, brand preference, and purchase intent. *Journal of advertising*, *24*(3), 25-40.

Fayrene, C. Y., & Lee, G. C. (2011). Customer-based brand equity: A literature review. *Researchers World*, *2*(1), 33.

Freund, J., & Jacobi, E. S. (2013). Revenge of the brand monsters:

How Goldman Sachs' doppelgänger turned monstrous. *Journal of Marketing Management*, *29*(1-2), 175-194.

Giesler, M. (2012). How doppelgänger brand images influence the market creation process: Longitudinal insights from the rise of botox cosmetic. *Journal of Marketing*, *76*(6), 55-68.

Guthrie, S. E. (1995). *Faces in the clouds: A new theory of religion*. Oxford University Press.

Holt, D., & Cameron, D. (2010). *Cultural strategy: Using innovative ideologies to build breakthrough brands*. Oxford University Press.

John, D. R., Loken, B., Kim, K., & Monga, A. B. (2006). Brand concept maps: A methodology for identifying brand association networks. *Journal of Marketing Research*, *43*(4), 549-563.

Kapferer, J. N. (2012). *The new strategic brand management: Advanced insights and strategic thinking*. Kogan page publishers.

Keller, K. L. (2003). Brand synBook: The multidimensionality of brand knowledge. *Journal of consumer research*, *29*(4), 595-600.

Krishnamurthy, S., & Kucuk, S. U. (2009). Anti-branding on the internet. *Journal of Business Research*, *62*(11), 1119-1126

Schnittka, O., Sattler, H., & Zenker, S. (2012). Advanced brand concept maps: A new approach for evaluating the favorability of brand association networks. *International Journal of Research in Marketing*, *29*(3), 265-274.

Sood Gaurav & Sharma J K, American International Journal of Research in Humanities, Arts and Social Sciences, 12(2), September-November, 2015 pp. 241-245.

Sood & Sharma., American International Journal of Research in Humanities, Arts and Social Sciences, 16(3), September-November, 2016, pp. 201-206

Sood, G & Sharma, J K. (2017). Measurement and Impact of Brand Doppelgänger Imagery on a Brand. International Journal of Applied Business and Economic Research, Vol. 15(17), pp. 241-251.

Thompson, C. J., Rindfleisch, A., & Arsel, Z. (2006). Emotional branding and the strategic value of the doppelgänger brand image. *Journal of Marketing*,*70*(1), 50-64.

Vardoulakis, D. (2004). The critique of loneliness: Towards the political motives of the doppelgänger. *Angelaki: Journal of the Theoretical Humanities*, *9*(2), 81–101.

❒

MEASUREMENT & IMPACT OF BRAND DOPPELGÄNGER IMAGERY ON A BRAND

Gaurav Sood
Faculty of Management Studies, Manav Rachna Institute of Research & Studies
and
J K Sharma
Amity Business School, Amity University

ABSTRACT

Managing a brand image and brand equity has been of paramount importance for marketers and researchers alike. The Customers' perception of a brand impacts and influences the brand equity and acts as a decisive force in gaining competitive advantages. Brand equity and brand image are widely researched in existing research studies. Doppelgänger Brand Imagery holds tremendous potential in the existing literature review and needs to be studied in depth. Doppelgänger Brand Image comprises of negative perceptions that create a dominant or recurring concept that influence the performance of a brand.

Understanding after much thought brand equity involves deciphering the lattice of powerful, appealing, and unique brand linkages in the perceptions of the stakeholders (Keller, 2003). This paper captures the brand associations and network of those brand associations with respect to the Indian Premier League (IPL) by developing IPL's Brand Concept Maps (BCM) and Advanced Brand Concept Maps (ABCM). The process followed is to draw out the brand association networks (maps) from consumers and aggregating individual maps into a brand consensus map. Consensus brand maps include the core brand's positive and negative associations that define the brand's image and shows direct and indirect linkages of brand associations to the brand.

This paper analyses the problems in traditional ABCM, and modifies the measurement to reveal dynamics of impact Doppelgänger has on the brand measurement. The disparaging images of IPL are captured through negative brand associations and an analysis has been carried out to understand the impact of these monstrous negative associations on the overall brand imagery of IPL.

As explained in this paper, the dynamics on the brand are assessed at all levels: listing of impacting constituents, their relative importance, and the drift of their positive or negative influence, et al.

Keywords: *Doppelgänger Brand Image; Brand Concept Maps; Brand Monster; anthropomorphism; Cultural Jamming; Cultural Branding; Brand Image; Brand Associations.*

Brand *Doppelgänger – an overview*

Brand equity and brand image are widely discussed in existing studies (for example, Aaker, 1996; Keller, 2003). Professor Jean-Noël Kapferer in 1986 was the first person to come out with the concept of "Brand Identity". He developed a brand identity six sided prism model, which coherently explained the six aspects of brand identity into two dimensions. The first dimension talked about brand as a person and can be explained as brand physique and brand personality and also depicts user reflection and self-image. Second dimension explained a brand's social aspects; its physique, relationship and reflection incorporated into the brand personality, culture and self-image. Kapferer (2004) contends an opinion that, "Powerful brands have potency of knitting all N dimensions into an effective oneness to generate a precise, clear and likeable brand identity." Brand has been the center of attention for academicians and marketers alike – a concept admired and has generated various views and definitions. Brand has been defined as a network of associations in consumer's minds (Keller, 2003). High brand equity leads to strong consumer preferences and purchase intent (Cobb-Walgren et al. 1995), further strong brand equity leads to higher returns in stocks (Aaker and Jacobson, 1994). Keller (2003) though introduced the concept of customer brand equity; a conceptual framework to map customer based brand equity was further developed by Fayrene and Lee (2011).

Another powerful concept is anthropomorphisation (attribute the human form to nonhuman forms, characteristics or events which extend throughout human judgment (Guthrie 1993)); Aggarwal and McGill (2007) researched and developed a framework to conceptually understand anthropomorphisation of products. Their finding favored products that are presented as humans and have human like characteristics have positive consumer's evaluation. According to the anthropomorphisation concept a brand is seen as comparable to human, having characteristics similar to a human being. Brown's (2010) suggested that brand anthropomorphisation leads to a larger market share. This happens in a situation when the brand custodians anthropomorphized a brand to an animal, which is "closer" to humanity. However, Holt (2010) introduced cultural strategy concept, a cultural ideology that consumer relate to. This cultural strategy theory makes anthropomorphism of brand indefensible for the consumers. He discarded the mindshare strategies adopted by marketers and suggested innovative ideologies to build strong brands.

Keller (2003) studied the mechanism of forming a semantic / meaningful connect with a brand in mind of consumer. This image of brand gels into a network of associated unique and positive associations in the mind of the consumer (John, Loken, Kim, & Monga, 2006; Keller, 1993). The elements here are direct and indirect linkages. This lattice of connects acquires shape of a positive correlate of a brand's value to consumers (Aaker, 2010; John et al., 2006).

As companies try to promote their brands and establish positive brand imagery, alongside is created the Doppelgänger brand image i.e. the negative brand associations in the mind of consumers. The Doppelgänger as a dominant concept came from the German Romanticism and became a order of the the "Gothic" literature. Jean Paul first used in his novel Siebenkiis, published in 1796 (cited in: Vardoulaki 2006). According to Thompson et al (2006), "Doppelgänger Brand Image is a cohort of disparaging images and anecdotes about a brand that float around in popular culture by an amorphous network of consumers, anti-brand activists, bloggers, and perception leaders in the news and entertainment media."

Though the dark side of the brand is not researched much; mapping of anti-consumption and anti-branding has been done in the digital space (Krishnamurthy 2009). Why a strong Doppelgänger may lead to brand avoidance Lee (2009). According to Harold (2007) media activism used by pranksters have provoked the brand custodians. Giesler (2012) case study of Botox brand analysis analyzed the impact of Doppelgänger Brand Image on the brand. According to Thompson et al. (2006), strong brands are more vulnerable to the doppelgänger brand image confusing consumers and may lead to brand avoidance. According to Freund and Jacobi (2013): "The emergence of a powerful, popular Doppelgänger may signal that a brand has peaked and must either evolve or decline." In the backdrop of the Goldman Sachs case example, Freund and Jacobi (2013) through their study explained that how the anti-brand activists can lead to the creation of the Doppelgänger brand imagery and influence the perceptual positioning of the brand.

According to Thompson et al (2006), Emotional Branding leads to the creation of the Doppelgänger Brand Image. Contrary to popular beliefs, Vardoulakis (2006) has given a new dimension to the Doppelgänger brand imagery. According to him the Doppelgänger is not always monstrous but it can have a positive potential too. Brand Doppelgänger's positive facet is an interesting side of the concept and needs to be explored further.

Researches pertaining to brand image limit themselves to consumer perceptions (Lassaret al., 1995). Aaker (1996) has delineated ways to measure brand, indicating how such a complex construct like brand can be practically measured. Ways to measure Doppelgänger Brand Image have been discussed by Brandt et al (2010) by studying negative user-generated content. Schnittka et al (2012) have validated Brand Concept Maps (John et al 2006) as most appropriate measuring mechanisms.

Indian Premiere League (IPL) Doppelgänger

The measurement and impact of Doppleganger was tested on Indian Premier League (IPL), an international cricket league, tournament organized by and in India. Research studies have studied IPL as an international brand, Gupta (2011) has studied the evolution and growth of brand IPL, he explored the rise of the IPL model and how it was responsible for bringing India's influence over world cricket. He also cautioned about the controversial aspect of the league (financial scams, unethical match-fixing, nepotism, betting charges etc.) Cricket has been known as a gentleman's sport; however, IPL got bogged down in scandals of betting and match fixing, exposing the darker side of this famous sport. IPL's Doppelgänger Brand Image emerged thereon due to negative associations and publicity. Therefore, a deeper study into IPL's Doppelgänger Brand Image was the need of the hour. This study was carried out to gain a deeper understanding of the measurement and impact of the IPL's Doppelgänger imagery.

Key Question:

Can a strong IPL Doppelgänger lead to Brand avoidance?

Research Methodology

There are many qualitative and quantitative research techniques that could be employed to measure the impact on a brand, namely consumer mapping and analytical techniques (John et al, 2006). Out of these, Advanced Brand Concept Mapping (Schnittka et al 2012) comes closer as a consumer mapping techniques, which provides qualitative & quantitative approach for this research; and also unearths the various dimensions of the brand Doppelgänger. At first, Zaltman Metaphor Elicitation Technique (ZMET)

(Zaltman, Gerald 1997) was thought of as the appropriate methodology for this research. The initial assumption came out from Mehrabian's (1971) mentioning that 93 percent of messages are non-verbal. This was clear as Brand Perceptions emerge from both conscious and unconscious observations of the consumers. This is important especially when we talk about the Doppelgänger Brand Imagery, because the consumers may not express their negative perceptions openly. Also it is important to know that how negative association may influence negative purchase intent. Therefore, Brand Concept Mapping (John et al 2006) is much more appropriate research tool to measure the same. Since the research has to get deeper insights into the consumer perceptions, therefore personal interviews which are employed by this approach is much reliable.

Brand image refers to the strength, uniqueness and favourability of brand association, organized in a network (Keller, 2003). The only limitation of the Brand Concept Mapping approach is that it can only analyze the strength and uniqueness of the brand associations (Schnittka et al 2012). The psychoanalytic dimension thus gets due merit and attention. On the other hand, Advanced Brand Concept Maps factor direction of favorability of these brand associations, but wrongly show lower impact for low ranked favourable constituents.

The IPL consensus brand concept map included both positive and negative brand associations, as IPL is a popular sports event and also is marked by controversies like fixing, betting, black money etc. The respondents were not only influenced by the IPL live matches updates, TV programming, star players but also had a negative influence from the negative publicity arising from the IPL controversies. Also most of the respondent were youth and therefore were active on the social media. They not only generate content but also get influenced by the user-generated content on IPL. IPL has a almost 58:42 as ratio of positive and negative sentiments (30db.com as on May 5th, 2016) floating on the internet particularly the social media like facebook, twitter, YouTube etc.

The study was carried out over the following steps:

(i) Experts were asked to list various brand associations, which have impact on the brand IPL. Our sample in this was 30 experts very familiar with cricket and IPL people (critics, commentators, article writers, players et al). They thus revealed 25 brand associations. They also rated these 25 as positive shapers of the brand (called Positive Influencers – PI) or negative influencers (called Doppelgänger Influencers - DI), as pertinent.

(ii) Further the requirement was to analyze the Brand Association Network Value (BANV), in order to quantify the overall favorability of brand association networks. The BANV is based on multi-attribute attitude model given by Fishbein and Ajzen (1975), according to this model brand attitudes are a multiplicative function of the salient (cognitive) beliefs that a consumer has about the product or service and the evaluative (affective) judgment of those beliefs (Ajzen Fishbein, 1980).

Therefore, the next step included the individual brand association's favorability evaluation of an individual brand association network for consumer 'j' (i.e., BANVj) initially consists of the added evaluative judgments of all brand associations 'm' that occurred in the individual brand map, multiplied with the strength of each association linkages to the nodal brand or superordinate co-associations in the memory of the consumer (i.e., Reder & Anderson, 1980; John et al., 2006).

Respondents were asked to assign the 25 brand associations four values: E, S, I, and L. is the respondent j's evaluative judgment of each brand association on a one-item, seven-point Likert scale, where a 7 point means more favourable rating. Also, represents the weak, moderate, or strong strength of an association to its superordinate associations within the network, with stronger linkages producing a greater association impact on the BANV, extended to a 7 point scale. Whereas, represents the individual importance of the association to a purchase decision. Further, each brand association's level of placement within the network is represented by and transformed to a seven-point scale to match the measures of Eaj, Saj, and Iaj.

All of these were to range on 7 point scales, with 1 as least value and 7 as most powerful, whilst 4 was a neutral middle ground. Our respondents numbered 120.

(iii) A BANV was computed for every respondent as follows:

We neutralized E by making it unit value in each case. This allowed us to compare weights as per directional categories, factoring direction, but not its weight.

(iv) Apart from overall consolidation, separate BANVs* were found for:

(a) Positive Influencers that received higher than 4 E value – dubbed SPI (same)

(b) Positive Influences that received a lower than 4 E value – dubbed FPI (flip)

(c) Doppelgänger Influencers that received a lower than 4 E value – dubbed UDI (unchanged)

(d) Doppelgänger Influencers that received a higher than 4 E value – dubbed RDI (reversed)

(e) Aggregate BANVs were also found for SPI & UDI combined; and for FPI & RDI combined.

*The tables in appendix show the results.

IPL'S CONSENSUS BRAND CONCEPT MAP

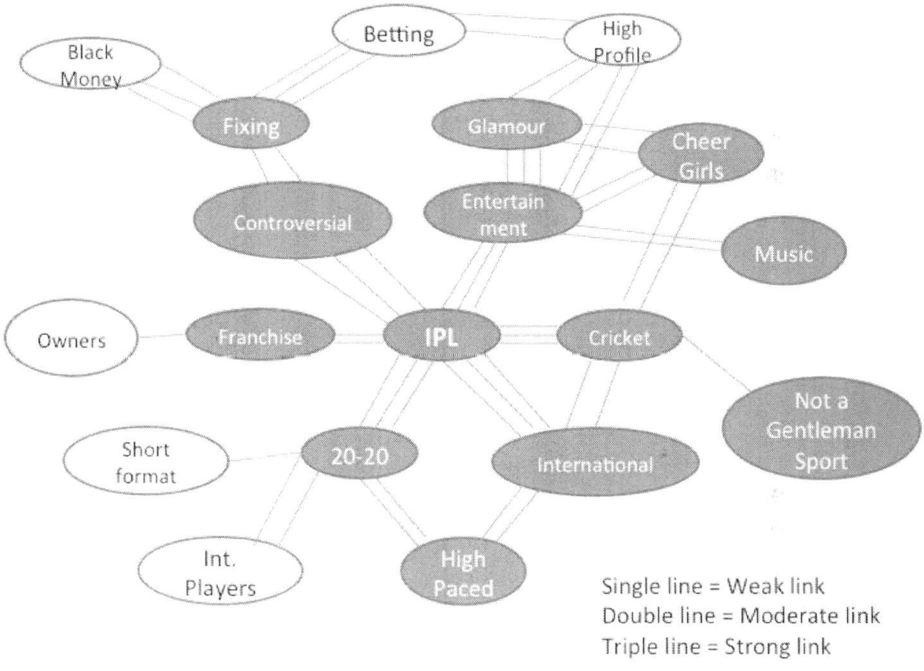

Figure 1.1

The favorability is illustrated in the figure I with the uniqueness and the strength of the IPL.

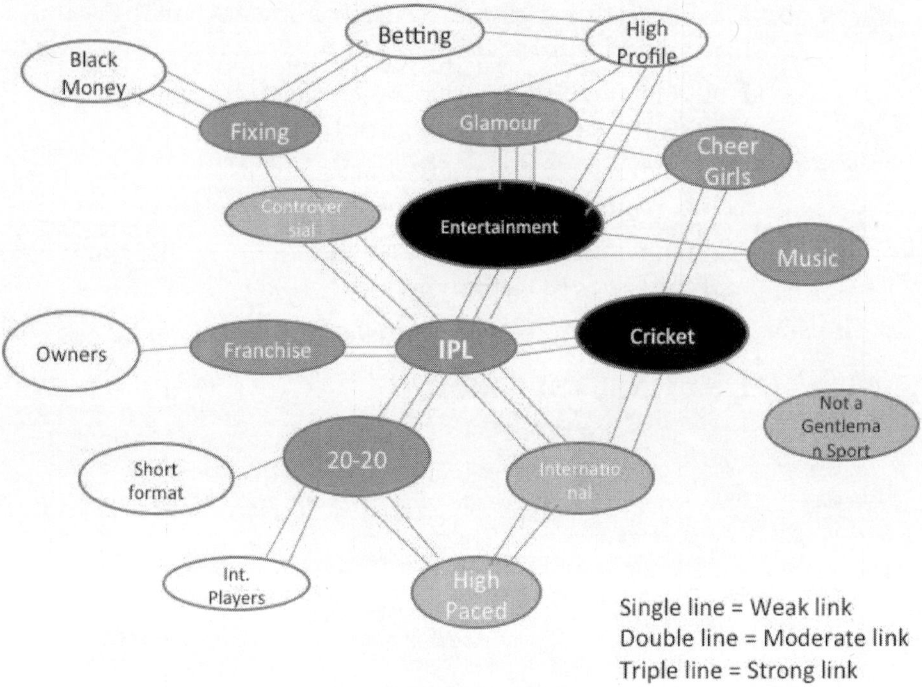

IPL Brand Concept Map with favorability

Figure 1.2

If we look into the map, we find that "Entertainment" and "Cricket" are the most favorable brand associations overriding the negative brand associations linked to the "Controversial" brand association. That means the respondents do not give much weightage to the controversies generated by the IPL like match fixing, betting and black money. This could be the reason of IPL brand going strong despite the Doppelganger brand imagery.

Analysis and Insights:

The following insights emerged from detailed analysis:

A. The way experts view a brand and the way general respondents can be very different. This is what accounts for change in status of Influencers. But it is the respondents who denote the consumer behaviour.

B. This is interesting, as it implies all so called Doppelgängers do not pull down a brand, and in a similar vein, the so-called Positive Influencers may not add to value of a brand.

   I. Overall IPL brand emerged with a BANV of 83.94.

II. The favourables gave a BANV of 134.99, which was 61% higher; the unfavourables returned a value of 36.82, which was 56% lower. This was in order with definitional standing of concepts.

III. The combined Positive Influencers (SPIs & FPIs) gave 102.62, showing the experts had gone wrong in assessment (as favourables got 134.9). Same ways the DIs combined (UDIs & RDIs) had 55.91, wrongly higher than unfavourables 36.82.

Conclusion

This paper exposes the imprecise brand measurements that have been hitherto made in many studies, as the analytic look into "real" Doppelgängers and "genuine" positive influencers mechanisms used to stay implicit. Also brand image measurement through brand associations network using Brand Concept Maps can only be limited to analyzing strength and uniqueness of brand associations. Whereas, to analyze an association's favorability to a purchase decision, it is only possible by quantifying the favorability of the brand association, through brand association network (BANV). Therefore we add the aspect of favorability to the existing BCM approach of measuring the strength and uniqueness of brand associations. By applying BANV, we are able to separate the "positive" and the "negative (Doppelganger)" brand associations by quantifying the favorability of the brand association network.

Further the marketing implication of this approach is that not all negative imagery or brand Doppelganger imagery leads to brand avoidance. Sometimes it even acts as a good monster and might impact positively to the brand health. Also as in the case of IPL the core motivation or favorable association to purchase decision is entertainment and not cricket. Therefore all the negative association like betting, match-fixing etc has less impact on the performance of the league as the consumer does not associate it with traditional cricket the "gentleman's sport".

This paper thus points out further similar measurement studies need to be carried out for other brands to see variance in judgment of critics/ experts and actual market representing consumers. It also gives insights into how a few Doppelgangers may actually be used to push up a brand, rather than treat all Doppelgangers as negative pull downers. Similarly, the classic view on positive influencers also needs a relook – as relative priority to be given to brand constituents may have a few positive influencers actually pull downers.

APPENDIX

Figure I – The favorability of brand associations

	1 = extremely low favorability; 7 = extremely high favorability	
S.No.	**Brand associations**	**Favorability**
1	Cricket	5.5
2	High Paced	4
3	20-20	5
4	Franchise	3.5
5	Music	4
6	Entertainment	6
7	International	2.8
8	Fixing	2.5
9	Glamour	3.9
10	Controversial	3
11	not a gentlemen sport	1.7
12	Cheer Girls	3.3
13	Format	3.7
14	High Profile	1.9
15	Betting	2.8
16	Star owners	3.2
17	International Players	3.5
18	Black Money	3
19	overdose of cricket	1.3
20	Parties	1.2
21	Contests	2
22	Conflict of interest	1.4
23	players conflict	1.3
24	Music	3.5
25	BCCI	2.6

TABLE II – THE 25 BRAND ASSOCIATIONS RANKED BY EXPERTS

Item Code	Brand Associations	Association Influence
1	Cricket	Positive PI
2	High Paced	Positive PI
3	20-20	Positive PI
4	Franchise	Positive PI
5	Entertainment	Positive PI
7	Auction	Positive PI
8	Glamour	Positive PI
12	International	Positive PI
15	Format	Positive PI
16	High Profile	Positive PI
19	BCCI	Positive PI
21	Star owners	Positive PI
22	International Players	Positive PI
23	Contests	Positive PI
25	Music	Positive PI
6	Cheer Girls	Doppelgängers DI
9	Controversial	Doppelgängers DI
10	Fixing	Doppelgängers DI
11	Parties	Doppelgängers DI
13	Players' Conflict	Doppelgängers DI
14	Not a gentlemen sport	Doppelgängers DI
17	Betting	Doppelgängers DI
18	Overdose of cricket	Doppelgängers DI
20	Black Money	Doppelgängers DI
24	Conflict of interest	Doppelgängers DI

TABLE III – AFTER RATINGS BY RESPONDENTS

Same PIs:

Cricket
20-20
Entertainment
High Paced
Auction
Franchise
Glamour
International

Table IV Unchanged DIs:

Betting
Not a gentlemen sport
Fixing
Overdose of cricket
Black Money
Conflict of interest

Table V Flip PIs:

International Players
Format
High Profile
Star owners
Music
BCCI
Contests

Table VI Reversed DIs:

Controversial
Cheer Girls
Players' Conflict
Parties

PIs = Positive Influence
Dis = Doppelganger Influence

Table VII – The BANVs

Overall	83.94
UDIs	44.26
SPIs	165.78
RDIs	73.4
FLPIs	30.44
UDIs & SPIs	113.7

RDIs & FPIs	46.06
UDIs & RDIs	55.91
SPIs & FPIs	102.62
Favourables	134.99
Unfavourables	36.82

References:

Aaker, D. A. (2010). *Brand relevance: Making competitors irrelevant*. John Wiley & Sons.

Aaker, D. A., & Jacobson, R. (1994). The financial information content of perceived quality. *Journal of marketing research*, 191-201.

Aggarwal, P., & McGill, A. L. (2007). Is that car smiling at me? Schema congruity as a basis for evaluating anthropomorphized products. *Journal of Consumer Research, 34*(4), 468-479.

Amit Gupta (2011) The IPL and the Indian domination of global cricket, Sport in Society: Cultures, Commerce, Media, Politics, 14:10, 1316-1325

Ajzen, I., & Fishbein, M. (1980). Understanding attitudes and predicting social behaviour.

Brown, S. (2010). Where the wild brands are: Some thoughts on anthropomorphic marketing. *The Marketing Review, 10*(3), 209-224

Cobb-Walgren, C. J., Ruble, C. A., & Donthu, N. (1995). Brand equity, brand preference, and purchase intent. *Journal of advertising, 24*(3), 25-40.

David, A. (1996). Building strong brands. *New York: The Free.*

Fayrene, C. Y., & Lee, G. C. (2011). Customer-based brand equity: A literature review. *Researchers World, 2*(1), 33.

Fishbein, M., & Ajzen, I. (1981). On construct validity: A critique of Miniard and Cohen's paper. *Journal of Experimental Social Psychology, 17*(3), 340-350.

Freund, J., & Jacobi, E. S. (2013). Revenge of the brand monsters: How Goldman Sachs' doppelgänger turned monstrous. *Journal of Marketing Management, 29*(1-2), 175-194.

Giesler, M. (2012). How doppelgänger brand images influence the market creation process: Longitudinal insights from the rise of botox cosmetic. *Journal of Marketing, 76*(6), 55-68.

Holt, D. B.. (2002). Why Do Brands Cause Trouble? A Dialectical Theory of Consumer Culture and Branding. *Journal of Consumer Research, 29*(1), 70–90.

John, D. R., Loken, B., Kim, K., & Monga, A. B. (2006). Brand concept maps: A methodology for identifying brand association networks. *Journal of marketing research, 43*(4), 549-563.

Kapferer, J. N. (2012). *The new strategic brand management: Advanced insights and strategic thinking*. Kogan page publishers.

Keller, K. L. (2003). Understanding brands, branding and brand equity. *Interactive Marketing, 5*(1), 7-20.

Krishnamurthy, S., & Kucuk, S. U. (2009). Anti-branding on·the internet. *Journal of Business Research, 62*(11), 1119-1126.

Mehrabian, A. (1971). *Silent messages* (Vol. 8). Belmont, CA: Wadsworth.

Reder, L. M., & Anderson, J. R. (1980). A partial resolution of the paradox of interference: The role of integrating knowledge. *Cognitive Psychology, 12*(4), 447-472.

Schnittka, O., Sattler, H., & Zenker, S. (2012). Advanced brand concept maps: A new approach for evaluating the favorability of brand association networks. *International Journal of Research in Marketing, 29*(3), 265-274.

Thompson, C. J., Rindfleisch, A., & Arsel, Z. (2006). Emotional branding and the strategic value of the doppelgänger brand image. *Journal of Marketing,70*(1), 50-64.

Vardoulakis, D. (2006). The return of negation: the Doppelganger in Freud's" The'Uncanny'". *SubStance, 35*(2), 100-116.

Zaltman, G. (1997). Rethinking market research: Putting people back in. *Journal of marketing Research*, 424-437.

❐

A HISTORICAL BACKGROUND TO GENESIS OF BRAND DOPPELGÄNGER

Gaurav Sood
Faculty of Management Studies, Manav Rachna Institute of Research & Studies
J K Sharma
Amity Business School, Amity University

Abstract

This paper maps the historical evolution of the concept of Brand Doppelgänger; tracking the emergence of earlier concepts of marketing, esp. brand. A better understanding of the brand and its imagery, equity of a brand, anti-branding and cultural jamming are necessary dimensions to understand the background to genesis of the doppelgänger brand. The paper explores the rise of anti-brand activities through user generated contents through the online medium. It further traverses the risk of emotional branding strategies and cultural jamming in creation of the monstrous doppelgänger brand imagery. This paper eventually puts together a strong case to either actively understand Doppelgänger power or work for brownie points at least. Therein, a defence of one's own brands against a Doppelgänger attack from competition or elsewhere is forcefully mandated.

Keywords: *Brand, Brand Marketing, Media, Brand Image, Brand Equity, Anti-Branding, Doppelgänger Brand Imagery, Marketing.*

Discovering Brand Doppelgänger

The world of marketing and brand et al has always moved fast, conceptualising the next high, or the next relevant concept idiom. This paper delineates the historical background that led to the genesis of the Doppelgänger concept. We investigate the literature on Brand, followed by Brand Image & Brand Equity, subsequently tracing Anti-Branding, concluding on Doppelgänger Brand Imagery.

Philip Kotler once described brands as helping people to make decisions. In a world of frenzied competition and bewildering choice, they are of course the fastest, simplest and most effective way to link a name to a perception of value. What can easily be overlooked however is that B2B and B2C brands are not just about very different types of decisions but that they also involve very different types of decision making.

For the most part, consumer brands look to influence an individual and/or groups of individuals (tribes). They are at their most powerful 'in the moment'. They are about excitement through identification, and they are often strongly influenced by culture, taste, fashion and what's important to people as people.

Two other insights are worth noting. The first: that the sense of value add is most important for publicly visible products and services, and that the importance of a strong and recognized brand increases significantly for those products and services that are clearly visible to the end user.

Brand – a complex phenomenon

Brand is a complex phenomenon. Though brands have been widely discussed and debated in academic world; a common understanding on brand could not be arrived at among the brand experts. "Each expert comes up with his or her own definition of brand or nuances of definition", stated Kapferer (2012), which increases the complexity in brand interpretation as well as its management. On the pivotal issue of how the brand strategies can be developed, Chernatony and Williams (1989), talk of two key components characterizing brands and through the use of a two dimensional matrix, thus identifying the type of brand.

Now brands need to be strong, for that is where business has competitive advantage. Hoeffler and Keller (2003) show how brand strength, operationalised in various ways, can create differential responses by consumers to various marketing activities. De Chernatony, L., & Dall'Olmo Riley, F. (1998) tried to define a brand. They content analysed over one hundred articles from trade as well as from academic journals, providing a broad and rich perspective of the range of definitions used. As a result of the content analysis of this literature, they identified twelve main themes which were an accurate categorization of the broad range of definitions of the "brand" in the literature, i.e. as: i) legal instrument; ii) logo; iii) company; iv) shorthand; v) risk reducer; vi) identity system; vii) image in consumers' minds; viii) value system; ix) personality; x) relationship; xi) adding value; and xii) evolving entity. The categorization into the twelve themes was fairly straightforward, since most authors used buzz words such as "personality" or "relationship" either in the definitions themselves, or in the discussion of their view of the brand.

This wrap-up of brand as a concept lay the earlier foundations, and helped marketing become more analytic via the construct of "brand".

Brand Image & Brand Equity

Branding is a complex concept and houses various other concepts like Brand Image and Brand Equity. A detailed understanding into the dimensions of brand image, bringing up four categories of functions: guarantee, personal identification, social identification and status is a useful study (A. Beln del Río et al, 2001). Dobni, D., & Zinkhan, G. M. (1990) have given a study, In search of brand image: A foundation analysis. A few pointers arise:

- Brand image is the concept of a brand that is held by the consumer.
- Brand image is largely a subjective and perceptual phenomenon that is formed through consumer interpretation, whether rational or emotional.

Brand equity is a vital facet of brand, and it originated in 1980s. Brand equity is closely related with brand loyalty and brand extensions. Therein arises the challenge of determining content and measurement of brand equity - whether financial or customer-based. The customer-based brand equity was studied by Chieng and Goi (2011).

Faced with absence of business-to-business (B2B) branding framework, Keller's customer-based equity model was tested for B2B context (Kerri-Ann L. Kuhn et al, 2008) - indicating higher emphasis for selling organization's corporate brand and its staff curability.

Keller (2003) enabled insights into various relationships that accrue, due to linking brands to other entities, for example, people, places, things, or other brands, as a means to improve their brand equity.

Thus the constructs of brand image and brand equity stood differentiated from the generic roots of brand. The need to define, and protect, and grow the brand, the brand image, and the brand equity took stronghold in the castle of marketing.

ANTI-BRANDING – From Activism to Hacktivism

Brand is no doubt a dynamic asset, it simply can't stay static. Thereby, its negative dimensions may flare up. In this linkage delving into theories of consumer resistance, and so coming forth with an alternative model, it has been shown that brands are authentic cultural resources. (Holt, 2002)

Hogg (1998) explored the phenomenon of brand avoidance, and its determinants. So as to keep brand flexible enough to remain workable. Further study by analysing qualitative data from 23 in-depth interviews, and introduction of negative brand promises idea was completed (Lee and Motion, 2009).

Antibrand behaviours have been observed to be diverse: from complaining to third parties, to negative word of mouth, to illegal actions such as theft, threats, and vandalism. Mapping was done as to conditions under which such relationships may be transformed into exceptionally negative dispositions toward once-coveted brands. (Johnson et al, 2011)

Light was shed on the learning processes used to negotiate brand meaning within an anti-brand community (Zinkhan, 2010). It was revealed the negotiation of brand meaning is a social process where community members engage in brand-related discourses, interpretations, and sense-making.

Anti-brand can't be completely said to have been studied unless the internet dimension has been covered. Web sites are online spaces that focus negative attention on a specific targeted brand. Anti-consumption movements on the internet have been gaining in numbers and in strength, research has not fully uncovered the nature of such sites and their impact on brand value and consumer anti-consumption. (Krishnamurthy, S., & Kucuk, S. U. ,2009).

The marketing's anthropomorphic propensity, via brand animals, mascots and icons is an interesting study which portrays advertising icon life cycle and four beastly branding strategies (Brown, S., 2010). Emotional branding is hugely in currency, even though this strategy is beset with many risks. Rindfleisch, A., & Arsel (2006) reasoned that emotional-branding strategies are conducive to the emergence of a doppelgänger brand image, which is defined as a family of disparaging images and meanings about a brand that circulate throughout popular culture. The primal Book they proposed was that a doppelgänger brand image can undermine the perceived authenticity of an emotional-branding story and, thus, the identity value that the brand provides to consumers.

Negative Double Jeopardy (NDJ) was researched by Kucuk (2008): that the most valuable brands attract more anti-brand sites while less valuable brands do not have such hate attraction on the internet. The NDJ phenomenon and the NDJ components [' Brand Rank ' and ' Brand Consistency '] were thus introduced. Negative publicity can lessen positive consumer perceptions of a brand – the holistic thinkers are less susceptible to negative publicity information than are analytic thinkers. Analytic thinkers are less likely to consider contextual factors, attributing negative information to the parent brand and updating their brand beliefs accordingly (Monga and John, 2008)

One of the stratagem in negative attack is parody. Measuring the consequences of parody on attitudes towards the brand that is the victim of the parody was studied (Jean, 2011). This study demonstrated that a brand parody communication by playing negative humour with an anti-commercial style represents a real threat for the brand parodied.

Going deeper in this arena, studies have mapped popular culture and modem communications media. It goes beyond mass media (Guillory, 2010). An across the spectrum exploration of cultural jamming was done from a point of view of developing a theoretical approach to explaining repertoire change and tactical choice (Iles, 2013). What came up was a rigorous conceptualization of culture jamming as an oppositional tactic.

Cultural jamming, a key part of negative branding, was linked to prankster (Harold, 2004). It was indicated the pranksters aren't revenge prone, instead they are on a provocative mode. 'Culture jamming' is defined as 'an organized, social activist effort that aims to counter the bombardment of consumption-oriented messages in the mass media' (Handelman and Kozinets, 2004: n.p.). Carducci (2006) took this further to fathom culture jamming from a sociological perspective, situating it in the 'expressivist' tradition, which originates with the mid-18th century thinker Rousseau and whose legacy extends to postwar Western counterculture.

The issue of hacking, a new kind of internet threat, was studied to show how disrupting communications using internet enabled networks and organizations was done. (Mahncke & Williams, 2009). The hackers are in a sense really hacking to support the hegemonic practices of their respective countries, and that this kind of activity represents a new form of civic participation in international relations.

A detailed history of hacktivism's evolution from early hacking culture to its present-day status as the radical face of online politics was laid out, along with describing the ways in which hacktivism has re-appropriated hacking techniques to create an innovative new form of political protest (Jordan & Taylor, 2004). The full social and historical context of hacktivism is positioned in terms of new social movements, direct action and its contribution to the globalization debate.

Cammaerts (2007) extended the cultural jamming techniques' appropriation by political actors in their political communication practices. These 'political' jams are not directed at the corporate world as such, like the cultural jam, but towards society at large or governments, towards changing values or behaviours and even at times against minorities or common enemies.

On the basis of semiotic theory mainly by Ferdinand de Saussure and Roland Barthes, study was made on the related issues of Culture Jamming as a social phenomenon, history of advertising, ideology and propaganda (**Önal**, 2005). Rumbo (2002) ingeniously showed reversing of resistance into an advantage - the obstacles inherent in launching challenges to consumerism, and the difficulty of resisting consumerism given advertising's control over cultural spaces were studied. It was shown how marketers have converted resistance efforts from some of consumption's most ardent critics into market segments by targeting certain goods and services toward them.

Shimp T. (2013) gave a revolutionary Book on pranking, illustrating how the yes man culture instilled culture jamming and carried tones of a disruptive rhetoric. Specifically, this Book poses many research questions, key ones being: What rhetorical strategies do the Yes Men use to critique dominant corporate discourse and expose counter discourses? A Foucauldian rhetorical analysis reveals that the Yes Men rely on pranks that employ satire and sincerity to disrupt dominant corporate discourses, open spaces of freedom, and encourage critical self-reflection. The strategies of the Yes Men offer no doubt important insight into the relationship between rhetoric, discourse, and activism.

Darts, D. (2004) in his paper, Visual Culture Jam: Art, Pedagogy, and Creative Resistance, argues that visual culture is an essential direction for contemporary art educators who are committed to examining social justice issues and fostering democratic principles through their teaching. The study explores how visual culture education can empower students to perceive and meaningfully engage in the ideological and cultural struggles embedded within the everyday visual experience. The work of resistance theorists and socially engaged artists, including culture jammers, is researched in an effort to support and inform the teaching and learning of visual culture.

This elaborate traverse of anti-branding provided the immediacy of the most analogous instincts in dangers besetting a brand; it was but natural for the concept of doppelganger to originate now.

Doppelgänger Brand Imagery

Abi-Ezzi, N. (2000) pores over the representation of the Double in the Work of Robert Louis Stevenson, Wilkie Collins and Daphne du Maurier. This is with particular reference to The Strange Case of Dr Jekyll and Mr Hyde', *The Woman in White,* and *Rebecca.* A rejection of the prevailing social order is the basis of this rejection, different in each case, that determines the context in which each treats the double. This psychological symbolism manifests itself in several themes - namely the representation of landscape, animals, masquerade and writing - central to the main texts, and relating them clearly to one another. This study, then, while contributing on one level to the comparatively sparse literature on Collins and du Maurier, expands an understanding of the motif of the double by filling a gap in existing criticism, demonstrating that it is to no small degree through the relationship of the double to a given set of themes, defined through psychological symbolism, that the course and fulfilment of its function are explained.

Aggarwal, P., & McGill, A. L. (2007) rub it in a satirical way when they query, "Is That Car Smiling at Me?" Their research proposes schema congruity as a theoretical basis for examining the effectiveness and consequences of product anthropomorphism. Results of two studies suggest that the ability of consumers to anthropomorphize a product and their consequent evaluation of that product depend on the extent to which that product is endowed with characteristics congruent with the proposed human schema. And thus consumers' perception of the product as human mediates the influence of feature type on product evaluation. Results of a third study, however, show that the affective tag attached to the specific human schema moderates the evaluation but not the successful anthropomorphizing of the product.

Giesler, M. (2012)'s paper: How Doppelgänger Brand Images Influence the Market Creation Process: Longitudinal Insights from the Rise of Botox Cosmetic, uses actor-network theory from sociology; and the author explores the creation of new markets as a brand-mediated legitimation process. Findings from an eight-year longitudinal investigation of the Botox Cosmetic brand suggest that the meanings of a new cosmetic self-enhancement technology evolve over the course of contestations between brand images promoted by the innovator and doppelgänger brand images promoted by other stakeholders. A four-step brand image revitalization process is offered that can be applied either by managers interested in fostering an innovation's congruence with prevailing social norms and ideals or by other stakeholders (e.g., activists, competitors) interested in undermining its marketing success. The findings integrate previously disparate research streams on branding and market creation and provide managers with the conceptual tools for sustaining a branded innovation's legitimacy over time.

Thompson, C. J., Rindfleisch, A., & Arsel, Z. (2006) comment on Emotional Branding and the Strategic Value of the Doppelgänger Brand Image. Emotional branding is widely heralded as a key to marketing success. They argue that emotional-branding strategies are conducive to the emergence of a doppelgänger brand image, which is defined as a family of disparaging images and meanings about a brand that circulate throughout popular culture. This article's Book is that a doppelgänger brand image can undermine the perceived authenticity of an emotional-branding story and, thus, the identity value that the brand provides to consumers. The authors discuss how the tenets of emotional branding paradoxically encourage the formation and propagation of doppelgänger brand imagery. They end up developing the counterintuitive proposition that rather than merely being a threat to be managed, a doppelgänger brand image can actually benefit a brand by providing early warning signs that an emotional-branding story is beginning to lose its cultural resonance.

Freund, J., & Jacobi, E. S. (2013) map revenge of the brand monsters: How Goldman Sachs' Doppelgänger turned monstrous. They found the analysis on cultural branding theory, brand psychoanalysis, and literary genealogy in a post-disciplinary manner to investigate the creation of an anthropomorphic, monstrous doppelgänger brand image by critics of Goldman Sachs. The case study explores how critics have succeeded in morphing the image of the bank into a 'brand monster' for a section of the general public. It is evident brand monsters focus negative emotions against organisations by exposing, anthropomorphising, and dramatising their alleged, monstrous, hidden motives, methods, and effects. This paper contributes to the literature on doppelgänger brand images by showing the importance of anthropomorphism when attacking a brand that does not employ emotional or cultural brand strategies.

Zivkovic, M. (2000) detours towards the Double As The "unseen" Of Culture, and evolves a definition Of Doppelganger. Despite a considerable interest in the fictional double, as a literary device for articulating the experience of self-division, the motif of the double seems to resist narrow categorization and definition. The starting position in the attempt to arrive at a comprehensive definition is founded on the assumption that the fictional double is not a literary motif but a construction of traditional culture – myth, legend and religion. Although surviving as a perennial motif present in all literary styles, periods and genres the double is never "free" – it is not "outside" time but produced within and determined by its social context. Through the introduction of some modern psychoanalytic theories, it has been possible to claim for the double motif a subversive function. Signifying a desire to be reunited with a lost centre of personality the double shows in graphic forms a tension between the "laws of human society" and the resistance of the unconscious mind to these laws. By attempting to transform the relations between the imaginary and the symbolic, the double hollows out the real, revealing its absence, its great other, its unspoken and its unseen.

Vardoulakis, D. (2006) elaborates Negation, going onto the Doppelgänger in Freud's "The 'Uncanny'". The Doppelgänger as a motif arose within German Romanticism and became a canonical theme in "Gothic" literature. The term was coined by Jean Paul in his novel *Siebenkäs*, published in 1796. Authors such as E.T.A. Hoffmann and Edgar Alan Poe exemplify the original narratives of the motif and theme of the Doppelgänger. Doppelgänger characters tend to be associated with evil and the demonic; thus one can infer that the Doppelgänger presents a notion of the subject/subjectivity that is defective, disjunct, split, threatening, spectral. With the rise of psycho-analysis, such epithets are taken to indicate a tendency toward a sense of failure or loss in the self. Thereafter, the Doppelgänger has been commonly viewed as an aberration, the stencil of a symptomatology of the self. Admittedly, psychological symptoms or forms of subjective failure can be inferred in the literary instances of the Doppelgänger. However, the Doppelgänger retains the potential to be articulated in positive terms. But this can only come to light by questioning the unproblematic equating of content – either as the plot of the story, or as the history of a self – with a stable and retrievable origin. When the notion of origin is no longer a simple "content," then the Doppelgänger can be allowed to make a contribution toward an ontology of the subject. The subjective ontology that the Doppelgänger introduces should not be seen as positing an original substance or essence. On the contrary, its formal openness allows for its own interruption. At the same time, that openness is impossible without the interruption. The Doppelgänger, then, is a form of relationality that is not only a condition of possibility, but also a reflection of and on that condition. In this way, the Doppelgänger is aligned to a notion of modernity as interruption.

Conclusion

As intended, this paper has most systematically laid down leading concepts, from bedrock of which the doppelganger has emerged. The objective thus attained is one, better communicating that a doppelganger is a look-alike **or double of a living person, sometimes portrayed as a** paranormal **phenomenon, or in branding terms one›s ‹double-goer› as an** evil twin has been attained. And two, with such a foredrop, a superior appreciation of what this concept stands for. With such fodder in hand, it is expected the analysts and custodians of brands in the corporate and social matrix, are beware of havoc that can be wreaked by manipulating the Doppelgänger identity. This should inspire and provoke thoughts on counter-measures, which is a natural subject matter for further studies. It is hoped, further studies plug in any gaps thus shown in the evolution of body knowledge around the mentioned concepts. In fact, another paper that focuses on Brand Measurement aspects would have extensive supplemental value.

References

-Abi-Ezzi, N. (2000). *An analysis of the treatment of the double in the work of Robert Louis Stevenson, Wilkie Collins, and Daphne du Maurier* (Doctoral dissertation, King›s College London (University of London)).

-Aggarwal, P., & McGill, A. L. (2007). Is that car smiling at me? Schema congruity as a basis for evaluating anthropomorphized products. *Journal of Consumer Research*, 34(4), 468-479.

-Allison R. Johnson, Maggie Matear, Matthew Thomson (2011) "A Coal in the Heart: Self-Relevance as a Post-Exit Predictor of Consumer Anti-Brand Actions", Journal of Consumer Research Jun 2011, 38 (1) 108-125.

-Beln del Río, Rodolfo Vázquez, Víctor Iglesias, (2001) "The effects of brand associations on consumer response", Journal of Consumer Marketing, Vol. 18 Iss: 5, pp.410 – 425

-Brown, S. (2010). Where the wild brands are: Some thoughts on anthropomorphic marketing. *The Marketing Review, 10*(3), 209-224

-Cammaerts, B. (2007). Jamming the political: beyond counter-hegemonic practices. *Continuum, 21*(1), 71-90.

-Chieng Fayrene Y.L. and Goi Chai Lee (2011) Customer-based brand equity: a literature review. Journal of Arts Science & Commerce, Vol.– II, Issue –1,January 2011.

-Darts, D. (2004). Visual culture jam: Art, pedagogy, and creative resistance. *Studies in Art Education*, 313-327.

-De Chernatony, L., & Dall'Olmo Riley, F. (1998). Defining a" brand": Beyond the literature with experts' interpretations. *Journal of Marketing Management,14*(5), 417-443.

-Dobni, D., & Zinkhan, G. M. (1990). In search of brand image: A foundation analysis. *Advances in consumer research*, *17*(1), 110-119.

-Freund, J., & Jacobi, E. S. (2013). Revenge of the brand monsters: How Goldman Sachs' doppelgänger turned monstrous. *Journal of Marketing Management*, *29*(1-2), 175-194.

-Giesler, M. (2012). How doppelgänger brand images influence the market creation process: Longitudinal insights from the rise of botox cosmetic. *Journal of Marketing*, *76*(6), 55-68.

-Guillory, F. (2010). Communication as Culture: Essays on Media and Society. *Journalism and Mass Communication Quarterly*, *87*(1), 199.

-Harold, C. (2004). Pranking rhetoric:"Culture jamming" as media activism. *Critical Studies in Media Communication*, *21*(3), 189-211.

-Hearn, K., Mahncke, R. J., & Williams, P. A. (2009, December). Culture jamming: from activism to hacktivism. In *Australian Information Warfare and Security Conference* (p. ٣).

-Hollenbeck C.R., Zinkhan G.M. (٢٠١٠), Anti-brand communities, negotiation of brand meaning, and the learning process: The case of Wal-Mart *Consumption Markets and Culture*, 13 (3) , pp. 325-345.

-Holt, D. B.. (2002). Why Do Brands Cause Trouble? A Dialectical Theory of Consumer Culture and Branding. *Journal of Consumer Research*, *29*(1), 70–90.

-Iles III, D. M. (2013). *The Contentious Performances of Culture Jamming: Art, Repertoires of Contention, and Social Movement Theory* (Doctoral dissertation, Louisiana State University).

-Jordan, T., & Taylor, P. A. (2004). Hacktivism and Cyberwars.

Kapferer, J. N. (2012). *The new strategic brand management: Advanced insights and strategic thinking*. Kogan page publishers.

-Keller, K.L. (2003), Brand SynBook: The Multidimensionality of Brand Knowledge, Journal of Consumer Research Mar 2003, 29 (4) 595-600.

-Kerri Ann L. Kuhn, Frank Alpert, Nigel K. Ll. Pope, (2008) "An application of Keller's brand equity model in a B2B context", Qualitative Market Research: An International Journal, Vol. 11 Iss: 1, pp.40 – 58

-Kozinets, R. V., & Handelman, J. M. (2004). Adversaries of consumption: Consumer movements, activism, and ideology. *Journal of consumer research, 31*(3), 691-704.

-Krishnamurthy, S., & Kucuk, S. U. (2009). Anti-branding on the internet. *Journal of Business Research, 62*(11), 1119-1126.

-Kucuk, S. U. (2008). Negative double jeopardy: the role of anti-brand sites on the internet. *Journal of Brand Management, 15*(3), 209-222.

-Michael S. W. Lee, Denise Conroy, and Judith Motion (2009) ,"Brand Avoidance: a Negative Promises Perspective", in NA - Advances in Consumer Research Volume 36, eds.

-Monga, A. B., & John, D. R. (2008). When does negative brand publicity hurt? The moderating influence of analytic versus holistic thinking. *Journal of Consumer Psychology, 18*(4), 320-332.

-Önal, B. (2005). *Subvertising Versus Advertising: A Semiotical Analysis of the Culture Jamming Act* (Doctoral dissertation, BİLKENT UNIVERSITY).

-Rumbo, J. D. (2002), Consumer resistance in a world of advertising clutter: The case of *Adbusters*. Psychol. Mark., 19: 127–148.

-Shimp, T. (2013). *The politics of pranking: the Yes Men culture jamming and disruptive rhetoric* (Doctoral dissertation, California State University, Chico).

-Thompson, C. J., Rindfleisch, A., & Arsel, Z. (2006). Emotional branding and the strategic value of the doppelgänger brand image. *Journal of Marketing,70*(1), 50-64.

-Vardoulakis, D. (2006). The return of negation: the Doppelganger in Freud's" The'Uncanny'". *SubStance, 35*(2), 100-116.

-Zivkovic, M. (2000). The Double As The" unseen" Of Culture: Toward A Definition Of Doppelganger.

❒

IPL BRANDENSTEIN - CREATION OF A MONSTROUS DOPPELGÄNGER IMAGERY

Gaurav Sood
Faculty of Management Studies, Manav Rachna Institute of Research & Studies

J K Sharma
Amity Business School, Amity University

Abstract

Doppelgänger Brand Image is a nouveau construct in the studies of brands and brand values. It maps negative perceptions, which impact a brand, as retaliation to its positive persona. This case study traces origination of Indian Premier League (IPL), a powerful sports domain brand in India, and how it has been buffeted by its doppelgänger. The problems within (financial irregularities, match fixing scandals, nepotism, off-the-field conduct of players etc.) have been laid bare. The reader develops a good understanding of the drivers behind the formation of this brand's doppelgänger. The unmanageability of such a fearsome development has been treated akin to birth of a Frankenstein for the brand (Brandenstein).

INTRODUCTION

Amongst all the sports in India, the sport of cricket carries the maddening loyalty none else can dream of. It's the opium of masses – paralyses the country to a virtual standstill on days the matches are played. Most children and adults are hooked to television channels and websites and radio commentaries, watching the affairs ball by ball or at least tracking the scores on every over. Naturally, the clout, the wealth commanded is of an unmatched stature. The celebrity players earn leviathan sums through endorsements and participation in non-game events. Variously defined events flourish over the calendar year, the Indian Premier League nee the IPL, being a noticeably prominent one. Cricket has various formats, viz. Test Matches, One Day Matches (50-50 overs), and Twenty20 Matches

(20-20 overs by each team). In the 'Twenty20' game, each team plays 20 overs each. IPL is a Twenty20 overs format mega event lasting longer than a month – round robin eighty games or so are played, with an ultimate final game. Multiple differentiations in shape of practices, jargon et al are woven in the game. Global TV viewership is massive. Naturally, the sponsorships pulled in are humongous. The format of IPL, a new thing for India, took a cue from emulating the football clubs thought of England. Franchisees own the teams, where the players are picked by bidding. A player's pedigree decides the price he may command. The game allows entertainment of the highest order, with cheerleaders and display of a quick momentum sport, unlike the laboriously slow Test Matches or racier than the quick One Day Matches. The whole game lasts a few hours in the evening after office hours. It was supposed to be an ingenious invention, and the property soared in its value. Started in 2008, the IPL series and the brand was valued at 4.13 billion USD a year later. This grew exponentially. Naturally, with such a stupendous growth to fame, nobody could imagine IPL running into rough weathers and infamy.

UPSETTING REVELATIONS

March 28, 2015, the BCCI President (BCCI was the apex governance body of cricket, Board for Cricket Control in India) was affixed to his TV screen, closely following the story unfolding on major TV News channels, esp. on The Economic Times Brand Equity program about the IPL Doppelgänger – a disparaging imagery of the IPL brand circulating in the popular culture. The socially networked consumers and stakeholders at large were creating a negative imagery of IPL on social media by mimicking the IPL brand messages and spoofing the IPL controversies, which was in stark contrast to the IPL's promoted brand imagery. The President was a worried man; he picked his phone and called for a board meeting on Monday. He informed every member of the board about his concern and asked them to come prepared for a discussion. His concern was that cricket was historically noted as a gentleman's game; however, IPL stood mired in controversies of match-fixing and mis-governance, bringing to fore uglier aspects of the commercial event. These had given rise to IPL's monstrous Doppelgänger Brand Imagery. Brand IPL was a beautiful hybrid of cricket and entertainment – it made huge business sense. The IPL model was successful and instrumental in India's control over world cricket. Yet, the television program indicated there were concerns about problems therein (financial irregularities, match fixing scandals, nepotism, off-the-field conduct of players etc.).

BRAND IPL: MARKED BY CONTROVERSIES

The never-ending series of governance and transparency lapses had cumulatively contributed to the rapidly declining brand value of the IPL (**Exhibit I**). Packed stadiums, close finishes and big investments by corporates and Bollywood stars – the eighth edition of the Indian Premier League (IPL) was all these and more. Yet, brand IPL took a few hard knocks following a series of controversies. Result: decline of ratings and advertiser's interest. IPL, which was once considered an advertisers' delight — finally gave everyone financially associated with the event a big jolt. "IPL is essentially two things — cricket and entertainment. Going ahead, one has to reduce the distraction around sport. It is a sports league, and banking too much on entertainment is a very short-term strategy as it fades quickly. You just have to focus on making the cricket entertaining. Adding glamour just doesn't prop up the brand in the long run," said Santosh Desai, CEO Future Brands. Regular controversies have given a body blow to IPL, sliding its brand value by over $1 billion (Rs 5,500 crore) in the last five years. In 2013, Brand Finance pegged the value of the IPL at $3.03 billion (Rs 16,670 crore), an increase of four per cent from $2.92 billion (Rs 16,062 crore) last year, but still a far cry from the $4.13 billion (Rs 22,719 crore) in 2010. (**Exhibit I**).

Figure 1: Exhibit I-IPL Process

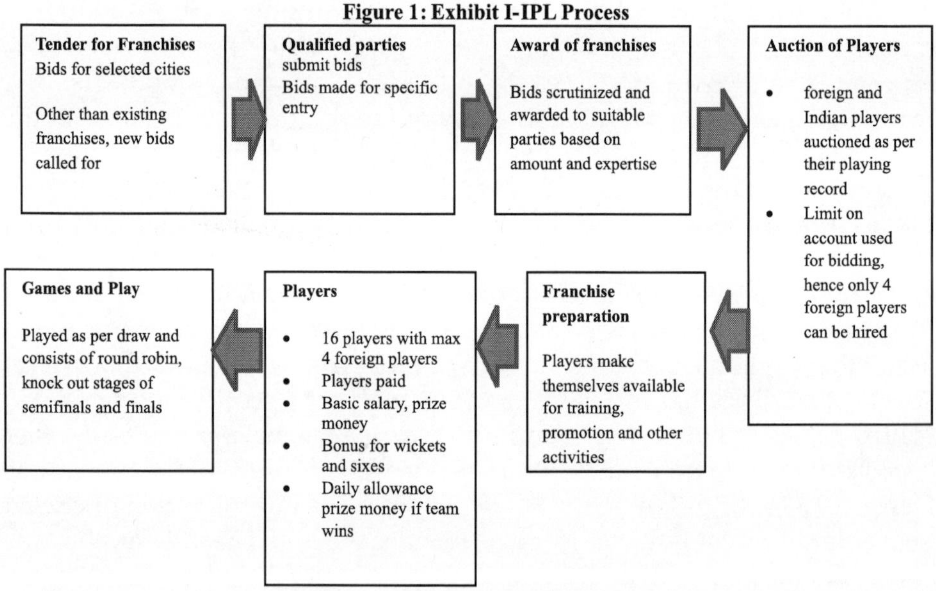

Figure 1: Exhibit I-IPL Process

Source: *Kapadia, Shashi (2013), "How sustainable is the strategy of the Indian Premier League - IPL? A critical review of 10 key issues that impact the IPL Strategy", International Journal of Scientific and Research Publications, Volume 3, Issue 12*

THE FALLING TRPS

Falling TVviewership is also a cause of major concern. TRPs (television rating points, a measurement of viewership) for IPL 6 had been on the decline in the last few years. IPL registered TRPs of 3.8 in season 6 as compared to its peak TRP of 5.5 in 2008 when the tournament started.In the current IPL season. IPL is in its Eighth season, and the analysts see it has reached a maturity stage. Brands which have been with IPL for the last seven seasons are coming back. Besides this few new categories are also adding to the list. With 70 advertisers and 12 sponsors, IPL-7 had at least Rs 1,500 crore riding on it, with ad revenues alone around Rs 800 crore from Rs 650 crore in the last season. In its eighth season, IPL clocked an average rating of 4.4 television viewership ratings (TVR) for the first five .matches against 3.1 TVR recorded in the previous season

EXHIBIT II: IPL REVENUE MODEL - A BIG MONEY SPINNER

Exhibit II: IPL Revenue Model - a Big Money Spinner

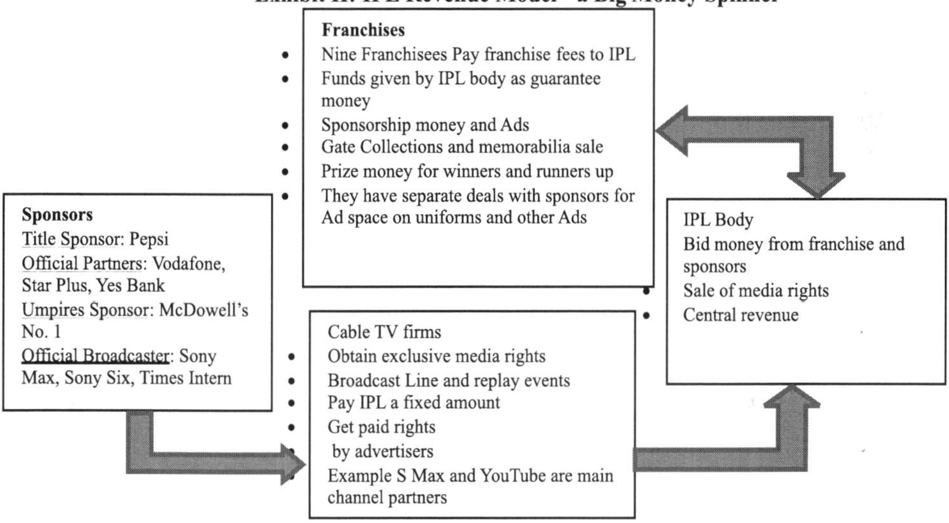

Source: *Kapadia, Shashi (2013), "How sustainable is the strategy of the Indian Premier League - IPL? A critical review of 10 key issues that impact the IPL Strategy", International Journal of Scientific and Research Publications, Volume 3, Issue 12*

TURNING POINT 2014

No doubt IPL was an interesting concept but the moot point was that some players took suborning and other unethical illegal means to supplement their earnings. The crime money always seems easy and additional. Last year especially rocked the game with match fixing scandals being proved and franchise owners questioned, which destroyed the ethos of a brand. Venality hits the probity, and is often taken unkindly by the viewers. They would naturally feel cheated on knowing the surprise element in the games was doctored, with rumours of as many as 100 aspects of every match having been pre-fixed, so that specific betters could win. This was anything like who would win the toss, who would bat first, what shall happen every 5 overs, the scores star players would max, which team would eventually win, by what margin, etc.

One of the key challenges for IPL is if the brand can last for the next couple of years, or a death knell had been irreversibly sounded. There is no point of a brand growing in the short term with a tactical entertainment packaging. There has to be repeat audience/viewers and a loyalty base developed across the nation in strictly marketing terminology. This is what IPL needs to monitor in the 2015 edition if one is to do justice to the brand that gave a new imagery to cricket and brand India.

BCCI PRESIDENT'S CONCERNS

The BCCI President mulled over the whole episode. The crowd had to be brought back to stadia. The advertisers' faith had to be restored. The TV slots had to be filled. The bidding process had to be made transparent. Ethics of players, by keeping them away from possible bookies had to be sanitized.

Essentially, he wanted the board member to discuss and develop strategy on Monday morning in that Stakeholders at large are using social media to exploit these IPL controversies. There were culture jamming messages and were creating a parallel imagery of IPL – The Monstrous IPL Doppelgänger. The stakeholders were employing Culture Jamming as a practice of criticizing and subverting IPL messaging and formatting in the social media (**Exhibit V**). The internet growth figures indicate that 30 million new users have been added since January 2014 alone, amounting to a 14% increase. Social media use is also growing, with Facebook alone adding one new user every second since January 2014. This digital growth is empowering IPL stakeholders to create IPL Doppelgänger imagery by way of social media backlash.

Next two days are crucial and filled with anxiety for the President. Hopefully he will find a solution to this social media backlash and manage the game in its full glory. And he expects the meeting called to brainstorm, and project a few feasible strategic solutions, that can impact fully counter the Brandenstein threat. This was akin to a Frankenstein raising its ugly head – a planned event getting out of control.

EXHIBIT III: IPL BRAND VALUE

					Game for Value Play
		Brand IPL Value: $ 3.03 billion (Up 4% from $ 2.92 billion in 2012)			IPL
					How the team stack up
Rank 2013	2012	Franchise	Brand Value 2013 ((Smn	Brand Value (mn $) 2012	% Change
1	2	Chennai Super Kings	45.42	45.28	05.
2	4	Kolkata Knight Riders	44.98	39.03	15.2
3	1	Mumbai Indians	44.62	48.21	-7.5
4	3	Royal Challengers Bangalore	37.81	41.15	-8.1
5	5	Delhi Daredevils	34.22	32.19	6.3
6	-	Sunrisers Hyderabad	31.49	-	-

Source:http://www.brandfinance.com/images/upload/brand_finance_report_ipl_v_league_table_final_04042013.pdf

EXHIBIT IV: IPL BRAND VALUE

Year	IPL Brand Value
2010	billion USD 4.13 $
2011	billion USD 3.67 $
2012	billion USD 2.92'$
2013	billion USD 3.03 $

Source:*http://www.brandfinance.com/images/upload/brand_finance_report_ipl_v_league_table_final_04042013.pdf*

EXHIBIT V: CREATING IPL DOPPELGANGER THROUGH IPL CULTURE JAMMING ON SOCIAL MEDIA.

Source: http://cartoonistsatish.blogspot.in/2013/06/acting-experience-in-ipl.html

Source: http://cartoonistsatish.blogspot.in/2013/06/the-ipl-match-between-delhi-and-mumbai.html

Source: http://ngelstalk.blogspot.in/2013/06/i-ndian-p-roblem-l-eague-its-atea.html

Source: http://indiatoday.intoday.in/gallery/cartoon-of-the-day/232/6301.html

Source: http://www.manjul.com/IndianCartoons/tag/poverty/

Source: http://indiatoday.intoday.in/gallery/cartoon-of-the-day/233/6301.html

Source: http://cartoonistsatish.blogspot.in/2012_05_01_archive.html

THE ISSUES TO BE RESOLVED

1. Can IPL reclaim its glory? What would be the action plan?
2. Is Doppelgänger an effective tool in hands of brand marauders/ raiders?
3. Are the brand derailers counterable or is their offensive unresponseable? Is their intent intermittent or sustainable?
4. What defences can any brand build against a possible Doppelganger onslaught?
5. Can these defences be proactively installed or are they only reactive?
6. Which lessons can the product brands and celebrity brands take from this episode?

REFERENCES

1. http://www.brandfinance.com/images/upload/brand_finance_report_ipl_v_league_table_final_04042013.pdf
2. Kapadia, Shashi (2013), "How Sustainable is the Strategy of the Indian Premier League - IPL? A Critical Review of 10 Key Issues That Impact The IPL Strategy", International Journal of Scientific and Research Publications, Volume 3, Issue 12.

❑❑❑